I Was Always On My Mind

*Are We Building His Kingdom
or Ours?*

Steve Sampson

Sovereign World

Sovereign World Ltd
PO Box 777
Tonbridge
Kent TN11 9XT
England

ISBN: 1 85240 170 2

Typeset by CRB Associates, Norwich.
Printed by Clays Ltd, St Ives plc.

Acknowledgements

Thank you Marilyn, my lovely wife, for praying for me and encouraging me, for listening to God, and for all your hard work and support.

My wife and I express a special heartfelt thanks to Fred and Betty Hicks for their painstaking work once again in editing another manuscript. May God reward your unselfish labor of love.

Contents

Introduction

This book highlights two specific areas of the Christian
life. The Jezebel spirit (the spirit of control) that has
attempted to cripple the church, and the power of the
flesh.

In explaining the Jezebel spirit, its history and how it
operates, I reveal a number of circumstances in which
controllers have operated with illegitimate authority, as
well as how the spirit of control functions through leaders
in positions of spiritual authority.

Additionally, I underscore the truth that God purposes
to dethrone every believer from the center of his own life.
He will return for a church without spot or wrinkle –
spotted by the work of flesh and wrinkled by self-will.
Blatant self-centeredness and selfishness are being dealt
with by the Holy Spirit in individual lives.

Ultimately, our flesh must be ruled by God and put
under subjection to the Holy Spirit.

Jesus was not on the earth to carry out His will, but to
fulfill the will of the Father. As believers, we must
renounce our own agenda and seek to fulfill His purpose
in our lives. The Holy Spirit is the Guide to reveal to us
His purpose.

All Christians must face up to the fact that their real
battle is with their flesh. The power of flesh, which is
capable of opposing the Holy Spirit in all He wants to do,

far exceeds the 'power' of the enemy. Jesus has already dealt a death blow to Satan! Now He desires to rule from the throne He has established at the center of our lives. All flesh must submit to His Kingship. He is Lord.

God's goal for each of us is maturity. He works with us to bring us to the fullness of His likeness.

> *'That we should no longer be children, tossed to and fro and carried about with every wind of doctrine, by the trickery of men, in the cunning craftiness of deceitful plotting, but, speaking the truth in love, may grow in all things unto Him who is the head – Christ.'*
>
> (Ephesians 4:14–15)

There is no question that we are living in a day when God is preparing the church for the greatest outpouring of the Holy Spirit ever witnessed before in history.

While my wife was in prayer recently, the Holy Spirit spoke to her these words, 'If the laborers aren't strong, the harvest will be spoiled.' God is raising up strong and willing disciples who will be instruments to minister strength and be able to disciple new believers into the fullness of Christ.

It's not what you've done, it's what you've become.

Chapter 1

I Was Always On My Mind

'For all seek their own, not the things which are of Christ Jesus.'   (Philippians 2:21)

Recently I was invited to speak at a Christian business-men's organization. A friend accompanied me to the meeting which was a little less than a hundred miles from where I live. The meeting was exciting and the word of the Lord flowed. On our ride home, my friend began to share about his experience that evening. He sat at a table (it was a dinner meeting) with five other men. During the meal he engaged each of the men in conversation.

He expressed his dismay on the drive home.

'Steve,' he said, 'I can tell you about the lives of each of these five men. I know what each one does for a living, how many children they have, how long they've lived in the area, and how they came to know the Lord. Yet in drawing this information out of each of them, not one of them asked me even one question about my life.'

I sympathized with his disappointment. I experience it all the time. Among unbelievers, I suppose it can be expected. Countless times, as I've been on flights, I engage the person next to me in conversation. He will talk about himself, his life, his job, his family, etc. for the entire flight and yet not ask me one question about myself. This is indicative of the spirit of the world and the spirit of this age. People's hearts are cold and often unwilling to take an interest in anyone but themselves.

But can it be that people who know the Lord and endeavor to live the Christian life, are still so bound to self-living and self-love that they don't yet have the maturity, or even the courtesy, to be mindful of the needs of others? If we are so self-oriented when we are among Christian brothers and sisters, how can we begin to think we can be an influence on the world? If our eyes are centered on ourselves, how can we be mindful that we are to be devoted to increasing the Kingdom of God?

There is nothing less becoming than self-centeredness. Those who are still under the delusion that the universe revolves around them are in a sad state. There is a saying, 'A man wrapped up in himself makes a very small package.'

In the past when I counseled an unmarried person, I would advise the young man or woman to ask God to send a mate who is a Christian and filled with the Holy Spirit. Now I counsel singles in an additional way – to pray for God to send them mates who have matured beyond self-centeredness, having learned to submit their flesh to God.

A term I heard frequently used during my early years as a Christian was that of self. 'That person is full of self,' I would hear the more mature saints say. What does it mean to be full of self? Self-centered people are totally consumed and preoccupied with themselves. Self-centeredness, self-loving, self-exalting, self-gratification, is their life style which eclipses any other need in the world.

Our Free Will

The gift God gives to every human being is that of a free will. Being born again does not guarantee maturity, any more than a child achieves maturity by being born.

Maturity is the willingness to lay our will and our rights at the feet of the King.

God will not renege on His gift to mankind. He will not override our will, but in fact will honor our freedom to make our own decisions. Even to the point of going to hell, God will not force any one to choose Him.

But maturity **is** choosing Him. Paul expressed his own progression beyond self-centered living in the famous chapter on love.

> *'When I was a child, I **spoke** as a child, I **understood** as a child, I **thought** as a child; but when I became a man, I **put away** childish things.'* (1 Corinthians 13:11)

God is Dethroning Us!

As Christians, we can rejoice over the fact that God has delivered us from sin. He has also delivered us from the vices of the devil and we can rejoice in the victory He has brought about in our lives. But now God wants to **deliver us from ourselves**!

It is wonderful to be saved from sin and know that our name is written in the Lamb's Book of Life. But it is possible to be saved and still be sitting on the throne of our lives. The truth is that we have been purchased by the blood of Jesus. Legally we have no rights to our new life. We are under His ownership! If we have really surrendered to Him, we can no longer sit on the throne of our lives. When we let Him rule we taste a whole new realm of victory. True freedom results when He is all in all, when He has title-deed to our lives.

We may be able to claim how God has used us in the gifts of the Spirit, or to lead people to Him. But we have to admit there are times we are laden with self-centeredness and impure motives. The Holy Spirit will reveal areas of our flesh that make us cringe. Yet, as we admit them and ask Him to cleanse us, we experience His taking us from glory to glory (2 Corinthians 3:18).

The Opposite of Love

If one poses the question of what the opposite of love is, a predictable response is 'hate'. But hate is only a symptom of the opposite of love. The most direct opposite of love is self-centeredness. Love is giving. Love is flowing out. Those who are self-centered only know how to receive. They are takers. They are self-willed, immature, and devoid of love except for themselves.

Paul spoke of this type of gross immaturity.

> *'But know this, that in the last days perilous times will come: For men will be **lovers of themselves**, lovers of money, boasters, proud, blasphemers, disobedient to parents, unthankful, unholy, unloving, unforgiving, slanderers, without self-control, brutal, despisers of good, traitors, headstrong, haughty, lovers of pleasure more than lovers of God, **having a form of godliness but denying its power**. And from such people turn away.'*
>
> (2 Timothy 3:1–5)

It is easy to write these types of people off as those totally poisoned by the world and its systems. But Paul mentions that many will have a form of godliness but deny its power. Could it be that this describes the state of many who profess to be Christians, but deny God's power to deliver them and bring change in their lives?

What good is an acknowledged Christianity if the flesh is still ruling and in control?

Feed My Sheep

The question Jesus posed to Peter three consecutive times was *'Do you love Me?'* Each time, no matter how Peter responded, Jesus said, *'Feed My lambs,'* and *'Tend My sheep.'* In other words, if you really love God, be mindful of someone other than yourself. Feed someone! Let your life pour substance into the needs of someone other than yourself. It is noteworthy that He doesn't say, 'Since you love Me, I'll meet all your needs.'

Although God is concerned with our needs, He is even more concerned with what is **flowing out** of us. He desires maturity that results in comfort, edification and strength to everyone we're in contact with. He desires that our lives be a substantial influence to everyone we meet, not because of our doings, but by the presence of God and His ability within us.

God desires to bring us to selflessness, wherein our life becomes a blessing and strength and 'food' for the benefit of many.

So many times I have heard people justifying themselves, claiming that they don't need to go to church, that they can seek God at home, or be spiritually fed from the electronic church. But church attendance is not merely for what you can **get**, but rather the cross-pollinating and the **giving out** of what the Lord has given you. Maintaining an idea that 'I can be fed at home' is nothing but pure ignorance and selfishness.

> *'A man who **isolates** himself seeks his own desire . . . '*
> (Proverbs 18:1)

> *'From whom the **whole body**, joined and knit together by what **every joint supplies**, according to the effective working by which **every part does its share**, causes growth of the body for the edifying of itself in love.'*
> (Ephesians 4:16)

Self-centeredness is nothing but blatant immaturity. Spiritual maturity means that we grow out of that selfish state into being mindful of the needs of others.

> *'We then who are strong ought to bear with the scruples of the weak, and not to please ourselves. Let each of us please his neighbor for his good, leading to edification. For even Christ **did not please Himself**; but as it is*

written, "The reproaches of those who reproached You fell on Me."'   (Romans 15:1–3)

*'For I say, through the grace given to me, to everyone who is among you, **not to think of himself more highly than he ought to think**, but to think soberly, as God has dealt to each one a measure of faith.'*   (Romans 12:3)

When Jesus warned Peter that He was going to be tested, He proclaimed, *'Simon, Simon! Indeed, Satan has asked for you, that he may sift you as wheat'* (Luke 22:31). But he also boldly proclaimed the **outcome** of the trial!

*'But I have prayed for you, that your faith should not fail; and **when** you have returned to Me, **strengthen your brethren.'***   (Luke 22:32)

Jesus knew the outcome of the trial was that Peter would be strong and able to strengthen his brothers. You can almost feel the excitement in the voice of Jesus, as He proclaims this reality – that Peter will be ministering strength. Virtue and encouragement will be flowing out of you, Peter! You will be a blessing to others!

God's Perspective

The mind of God is that He desires the **increase** of His Kingdom. When He blessed Abraham, it wasn't just for Abraham, but for **all** the descendants of Abraham. *'And in your seed all the nations of the earth shall be blessed'* (Genesis 26:4). When He gifts a minister to preach, it isn't to inflate his ego, but that souls might be won, and people might be blessed and strengthened.

When He baptizes believers in the Holy Spirit, He isn't giving a 'spiritual reward' or 'stamp of approval', but a gift that our lives might flow out to others. He has equipped us so that the gifts of the Holy Spirit might be manifest through us. He has in mind the countless people who will cross our paths during our lives. His Spirit will have access to their lives through our lives being a channel.

When a church is blessed with the need for a larger building, it isn't to reward the ego or performance of the pastor, rather it is a blessing from God that more people can be reached for His Kingdom. When He directs me to write a book, it isn't so I can boast that I'm an author, but that many souls might be encouraged and edified for His glory.

When God blesses the work of our hands, it is for the increase of His Kingdom, not ours. John proclaimed, *'He must increase, but I must decrease'* (John 3:30).

What Works Will Be Burned?

My wife and I had been meditating on Paul's words to the Corinthian church.

> *'Each one's work will become manifest; for the Day will declare it, because it will be revealed by fire; and the fire will test each one's work, of what sort it is. If anyone's work which he has built on it **endures, he will receive a reward**. If anyone's work is burned, he will suffer loss; but he himself will be saved, yet so as through fire.'* (1 Corinthians 3:13–15)

While in prayer, my wife asked the Lord what works will be burned. He spoke to her, 'Those created through men's minds, that are consequences of reasoning.'

Then she asked the Lord how we can know if what we are doing is an enduring work. He spoke to her three questions.

'Is Spirit-life breathed into it?'

'Did you pay the price?'

'Did you yield to your own initiative?'

Later He spoke another nugget of truth to her, 'When you yield to your own initiative, you cease being creative.' I thought about this and about how many adventures and awesome creative ideas we miss because we push on with our own agenda and do not wait for His initiative.

No More Agenda

There is no question that God is requiring that we live before Him to serve Him without our own agenda. For many of us we have determined to serve God 'our way' but as we mature we must acknowledge His Lordship and comprehend His words,

> *'I am the vine, you are the branches, He who abides in Me, and I in him, bears much fruit; for without Me you can do nothing.'* (John 15:5)

We don't have the luxury as believers of yielding to our own death-producing agenda. The only way to maintain God's agenda is to stay on His **supernatural airwaves**.

> *' "For My thoughts are not your thoughts, nor are your ways My ways," says the Lord. "For as the heavens are higher than the earth, so are My ways higher than your ways, and My thoughts than your thoughts." '* (Isaiah 55:8–9)

Jesus was our example. He lived without an agenda. His only purpose and desire was to say and do nothing except what He heard and saw the Father doing (John 5:19). He didn't come to do His own will and neither can we. We must lay our agenda at His feet and live in His presence, posturing ourselves to hear what He is saying. *'Man lives by every word that proceeds from the mouth of the Lord'* (Deuteronomy 8:3).

Flesh – The Way of Death

Recently the Lord spoke to me through a dream. In the dream I was observing some people who literally were at the doorway of hell. I stood amazed at how casually they acted, almost unconcerned about their place in eternity. I called out to a little girl, and said,

'You want to go to heaven, don't you? It is void of fire and torment and full of peace and joy.'

She hesitated momentarily and almost reluctantly verbalized a 'yes' and then slowly moved away from hell's treacherous entrance. As I stood there I could feel and smell the fumes coming out of hell's abyss. The only way to describe the fumes is that they reeked of horrible, nauseating hopelessness. Never have I felt such an appalling and hopeless emotion. A horrible feeling; no more hope; eternal anguish.

Then in the dream, an 18-wheeler pulled up. On the side of this massive truck was the huge word, JOKES. Over to the side there was a large group of 'yuppie' type people who were listening to a stand-up comic. I could feel an attitude emanating from them. It was as if they were saying 'As long as we are kept entertained and occupied, nothing else matters.' Clearly, the immediate gratification of laughter was more important to them than eternal matters. They were lulled to sleep by jokes, yet I knew it was the last chance for many. No one seemed to care or be conscious of the urgency.

The devil's strategy is to make a joke of all the important things in life, so that no one takes eternity seriously. Time is short. Christians must forsake passiveness and pursue the purpose of God for their lives. There is a world out there going to hell, which has been anesthetized by the 'entertainment' spirit of this world, whose hype is in the church body as well. It is time to seek the Lord. It is time to pursue His purpose for our lives and lay up treasures in heaven (Matthew 6:20).

I don't want to enter heaven empty-handed. I don't want to have to confess to the Lord on Judgment Day that I chose to live for **myself** rather than let Him birth His purpose in me.

Many believers have heard enough sermons to save

many continents, but to whom much is given much is required (Luke 12:48). We have heard so much we are inoculated from the urgency that eternity and eternal judgment await all mankind. Like the lyrics of the song by Andre Crouch, 'What'cha gonna do when you find out it's too late to get your heart right with God?'

Empty Vessels

When the prophet Elisha was sent to the widow who had been a wife of one of the sons of the prophets, she proclaimed,

> *'Your servant my husband is dead, and you know that your servant feared the Lord. And the creditor is coming to take my two sons to be his slaves.'*
>
> (2 Kings 4:1)

This woman had a valid problem, but Elisha saw it through different eyes. Fear and focusing her eyes on herself had paralyzed her. All she could see was her dilemma.

The prophet's proclamation to her catches us off guard, for we expect him to speak compassionately of how he was going to meet her need.

Instead he said,

> ' "*What shall I do for you? Tell me, what do you have in the house?" And she said, "Your maidservant has **nothing** in the house **but a jar of oil**." '*   (2 Kings 4:2)

Greater need than her lack of provision, was her paralysis. She needed to be **released**. Like the body of Christ, we are paralyzed with the fear of Satan robbing us. We call out to God to help us scrape by. Sometimes we are spiritually dry, and we don't understand why. But what we need are **outlets**! Through discouragement, we've turned our eyes totally inward, and we are in a quagmire of self-pity and self-centeredness. We need the oil (the Holy Spirit) Who abides in us to be released! The reservoir **already resident** in our lives needs to be liberated to flow to the needs of humanity.

The prophet tells her to gather vessels.

> *'Go, borrow vessels from everywhere, from all your neighbors – empty vessels; do not gather just a few.'*
> (2 Kings 4:3)

She was commanded to find vessels ... From her neighbors ... Needs ... A lot of them ... Don't think small. Start ministering to those empty people around you. The reason many are dry is because we have stopped pouring out the 'oil' that God has placed within us. Not to mention that we allow our minds to dwell on ourselves continually.

> *'And when you have come in, you shall shut the door behind you and your sons; then* **pour** *it into all those vessels, and set aside the full ones.'* (2 Kings 4:4)

Shutting the door is indicative of not telling everyone of your plans to begin to obey the Lord, or someone will talk you out of it. Just shut the door and do it.

> *'Now it came to pass, when the vessels were full, that she said to her son, "Bring me another vessel." And he said to her, "There is not another vessel."* **So the oil ceased.***'* (2 Kings 4:6)

What stops the flow of the Holy Spirit is when there are no more vessels. That is why we must seek God for a continual ongoing vision. Most depressed and discouraged people simply **lack vision**. They have ceased to pour out. No vessels (outlets) have been gathered and the flow of oil (the Holy Spirit) in their lives has ceased.

The key to always having something fresh from God, is to **never** stop pouring.

Self-centeredness is living without outlets. The word of the Lord to us is to get our minds off ourselves and gather vessels and begin to pour!

> *'Then she came and told the man of God. And he said, "Go, sell the oil and pay your debt; and you and your sons live on the rest." '*   (2 Kings 4:7)

When the Kingdom of God is preeminent in our lives (Matthew 6:33), the same oil we pour out to others will be abundant to meet our own needs. Repent of self-centeredness, which paralyzes, and seek for empty vessels to pour into. You will not be left empty-handed, but will experience the oil of the Spirit flowing through your own life.

How to Overcome Self-Centeredness

1.   A good gauge to measure self-centeredness is to look at your prayer life. How much do you pray? What percentage of your prayers are directed toward the needs of others and for the increase of the Kingdom of God?

   When we don't yield to prayer, it not only hurts ourselves, but 'clogs the pipes' for others who could have potentially benefited. A Christian not yielding to the flow of the Holy Spirit, is not only a non-participant, but a hindrance to the flow of God.

   If you realize you are praying only for yourself and your needs, repent. Then purpose to pray for the needs of others **always** before praying for yourself. *'Pray for one another, that you may be healed'* (James 5:16).

   A lady who had terminal cancer used to call us long distance for prayer. Although she was spending her own money on the call, and enduring great pain, she refused to let us pray for her until she prayed for us. She saw the principle of putting others first.

2. Make a habit of always asking people (with sincerity) about their needs before you talk about yourself. Look for empty and discouraged vessels. Unbelievers will respond when you genuinely show interest in their lives.

3. Ask God for opportunities to minister. Ask Him to show you who needs prayer or encouragement. Unselfish requests will be answered quickly!

4. Be responsive. Often the people who really have a testimony or a prophetic utterance to give, allow timidity or shyness to rob others of their gift. Therefore, others are robbed of their gift of encouragement from the Lord. As a pastor, I observed that shy people would often come up after a meeting and tell me (when there was no one around to hear it) of something God spoke to them. They were robbed, as well as those who would have heard the word of the Lord. When the shy don't yield, usually the strong personality-type people take over. They often have something to say even if God doesn't. Pray for boldness to overcome all timidity and shyness.

Many times in meetings, the Holy Spirit will begin to move and give words of knowledge specifically revealing needs of those present. Occasionally there will be instances when no one responds, and a heaviness settles in the room. Then later after the meeting, the person will approach me relaying how the word described him perfectly, but he was too timid to acknowledge it publicly. Again many were robbed of a blessing.

Shyness and timidity are rooted in preoccupation with self. It can be overcome.

Prison Escape

A wonderful example of selflessness is shown by Paul in Acts 16 when he and Silas were thrown in prison. When at midnight they began to sing unto God, it caused an earthquake forcing the prison's foundation to shake. As everyone's chains were loosed and the doors came open, they had a chance to make a run for it. But Paul wasn't thinking of himself.

Paul couldn't have seen with his physical eyes what was happening.

> *'And the keeper of the prison, awaking from sleep and seeing the prison doors open, supposing the prisoners had fled, drew his sword and was about to kill himself.'*
> (Acts 16:27)

> *'But Paul called with a loud voice, saying, "Do yourself no harm, for we are all here."'*
> (Acts 16:28)

Because of Paul's selflessness and compassion for people, he 'saw' by the Holy Spirit the entire scenario of the jailer committing suicide, and loudly proclaimed in the darkness for him not to harm himself.

As a result, the jailer came to Christ as did his entire household (Acts 16:31). All because Paul was living beyond self-centeredness.

Doing Your Own Thing

Many people, although saved, are doing their own thing for God. Without a prayer life, there will be no awareness of what the Lord is saying, and passivity and lukewarmness will take over.

Some evangelists book meetings without even consulting with the Lord whether He is specifically telling them to go to a certain city. God wants more intimacy than this. We have to decide if it is **our** ministry or **His** ministry.

Jesus was not on the earth to carry out His will, but to fulfill the will of the Father. As believers, we must renounce our own agenda and seek to fulfill His purpose in our lives. The Holy Spirit is the Guide to reveal to us His purpose.

Chapter 2

Flesh on the Throne

- It's not what you've done, it's what you've become.

It was in the early fall when my wife and I flew to Los Angeles to attend the World Full Gospel Businessmen's convention. We were both looking forward to being in the convention, as well as getting away from the responsibilities of pastoring for a few days.

However, I had an additional agenda. I was going to pour out my heart to God, and get some answers about some of my present unhappiness. There was no doubt in my mind that upon arriving in California, God and I were going to talk and He was going to deliver me from all my circumstances.

The first morning in California, I set the alarm early and set out for a long walk, and began to pray. With bitterness, I poured out my soul to the Lord, demanding answers for the unhappiness in several areas of my life. I hadn't delved five minutes into the prayer when in the deepest part of my spirit, a song began to arise. The words were crystal clear, as was the melody God was birthing in me at that moment. The words flowed,

'Jesus, Jesus, set me free,
The problem's not in people,
the problem is in me.

Jesus, Jesus, set me free,
The problem is not in anyone else,
the problem is in me.'

Verses to the song followed:

'I walked through life,
indignantly,
Seeking to have my own way,
But Jesus said, "Face yourself"
And the truth set me free that day.'

I didn't feel like singing, but I didn't have a choice. The sweet Holy Spirit was confronting my flesh. He was clearly declaring that my frustrations and discontentments were from my own flesh, and not the fault of any person or any circumstance.

Although grateful to hear the Lord's voice, this wasn't what I wanted to hear. I wanted the Lord to sympathize with me and promise me deliverance from all my situations and the people who made my life difficult. I wanted justice and understanding.

But God did understand, and was gently pointing out that it was all rooted in me. This has always been the hardest part of my Christian life – admitting that I'm the problem. In fact, it doesn't even help to blame the devil in most cases. God isn't struggling with the devil, rather His desire is that our will (our willful and powerful flesh), be in submission to His Spirit. He purposes to dethrone each of us from the center of our lives, and to be Lord.

But there is a power all Christians must contend with, the power of human flesh. The power of flesh does more to hinder the work of God than any evil spirit could begin to take credit for.

God's Goal

We constantly hear talk about the devil, but let's put the

devil in his place. The devil is a defeated foe; Jesus Christ has placed him under **our** feet.

He's a deceiver. He doesn't work through power; he works through **deception**. To fight the devil, we don't need more power; we need more light. When light comes, darkness flees.

Jesus only attributed to the devil one thing – that he is a liar. '... *When he speaks a lie, he speaks from his own resources, for he is a liar and the father of it'* (John 8:44).

God's objective and desire is that He sit on the throne of our individual lives, and that He rule as King and Lord in us personally. The devil is not the issue, as much as the power of our flesh, and the strength of our human will. The devil works to deceive, but God desires to take us into maturity.

God's purpose is to bring us to maturity above all else.

> '*Till we all come to the unity of the faith and of the knowledge of the Son of God, to a **perfect man**, to the measure of the stature of the fullness of Christ; that we should no longer be children, tossed to and fro and carried about with every wind of doctrine, by the trickery of men, in the cunning craftiness of deceitful plotting.*'　　　　　　　　　　(Ephesians 4:13–14)

Although at one time I blamed the devil for everything, my perspective has completely changed. I now can resist a small and defeated devil, and serve a big God. Although we must rebuke and resist the devil, we also must acknowledge that he is under the feet of every believer (Luke 10:19) and should only be someone we kick around. A football-size devil. My toughest battle is with my flesh, and by God's grace I can keep it in subjection to the Holy Spirit.

> '*For if you live according to the flesh you will die; but if **by the Spirit** you put to death the deeds of the body, you will live.*'　　　　　　　　　　(Romans 8:13)

What Happened at the Cross?

It was at the cross where the devil was stripped of his authority. Through the cross God dealt the death blow to Satan, inflicting an eternal and irreversible defeat on him. He is a defeated foe. He has been bound. The victory has been won by Jesus. However, although the victory is won, it is up to us to administer the victory.

Jesus said it plainly,

> '*All authority has been given to Me in heaven and on earth. Go therefore and make disciples of all the nations...*' (Matthew 28:18–19)

Since the devil is defeated, he only has one strategy remaining, which is to **blind the eyes** of the believers to the fact that he is already defeated, and thus prevent them from using their God-given authority available to them to overcome.

Paul addresses a group of these victims to the blindness given by the enemy.

> '*O foolish Galatians! Who has **bewitched** you that you should not obey the truth, before whose eyes Jesus Christ was clearly portrayed among you as crucified? This only I want to learn from you: Did you receive the Spirit by the works of the law, or by the hearing of faith? Are you so foolish? Having begun in the Spirit, are you now being **made perfect by the flesh**? Have you suffered so many things in vain – if indeed it was in vain? Therefore He who supplies the Spirit to you and works miracles among you, does He do it by the works of the law, or by the hearing of faith?*' (Galatians 3:1–5)

This group of people had seen it all. They were born again, had received the Holy Spirit, seen miracles, yet they were bewitched.

They had lost sight of the cross! Trying to please God with works (rules and regulations) obscures and eclipses the cross.

The devil wants to veil and cloud the cross, because that is where he was defeated. If he can diminish the cross in our life, he can get back in control. This happens when believers, forgetting the cross, get back under the law (*'Did you receive the Spirit by the works of the law?'*) relying on legalism, which is relying on flesh instead of the Spirit.

The law and the flesh are married. If anyone tries to justify himself by legalism, he is back in the flesh. At the cross our old man died, and we were delivered from the law and married to Christ. Without seeing the cross, which is grace through faith, legalism becomes the only other alternative – do it yourself, by your works. Legalism not only brings people back under slavery, but back under a **curse** from which we have been redeemed. But the just shall live by faith.

We are under a curse if we are depending upon the arm of the flesh. *'Cursed is the man who trusts in man and makes flesh his strength, whose heart departs from the Lord'* (Jeremiah 17:5).

When people begin to trust the flesh, the product of the work of their hands, their do's and don'ts, what they wear, their credit cards, their special friends, their mailing list, even their reputation, etc., they are under a curse.

When people are trusting in other things (even religious things) their hearts are turned away from the Lord, and thus they are under a curse.

What About the Law?

Many people become confused about the law. Some reject it, saying, 'We are not under the law,' implying we can live lawlessly. Others spend all their time emphasizing the law.

Jesus did not throw away the law! He fulfilled it!

> *'Do not think that I came to destroy the Law or the Prophets. I did not come to destroy but to fulfill. For assuredly, I say to you, till heaven and earth pass away, one jot or one tittle will by no means pass from the law until all is fulfilled.'* (Matthew 5:17)

But then He **abolished it as a means** for us to approach God and be reckoned justified, innocent and righteous.

In fact, the Scripture plainly says that if we try to use the law to be justified, we are living under a curse.

> *'For as many as are of the works of the law are under the curse, for it is written, "Cursed is everyone who does not continue in all things which are written in the book of the law to do them." But that **no one is justified by the law in the sight of God** is evident, for "the just shall live by faith."'* (Galatians 3:10–11)

But Jesus has made a way for us to be redeemed from the curse.

> *'Christ has redeemed us from the curse of the law, having become a curse for us (for it is written, "Cursed is everyone who hangs on a tree").'* (Galatians 3:13)

Trying to live by the law obscures Calvary, and separates us from the Lord.

> *'You have become estranged from Christ, **you who attempt to be justified by law**; you have fallen from grace.'* (Galatians 5:4)

What About the Devil?

The devil is a deceiver. Frankly, far too much attention is accorded to him by Christians.

Isaiah spoke of the remorse of many who expended so

much energy fighting a 'small' and defeated foe. He is **now** under our feet.

> *'Those who see you will gaze at you, and consider you, saying: "Is this the man who made the earth tremble, who shook kingdoms, who made the world as a wilderness and destroyed its cities, who did not open the house of his prisoners?"'* (Isaiah 14:16–17)

Doctrinally, Satan has been stripped of all his power and ability to inflict harm upon the saints. Jesus has disarmed him of all power and authority.

> *'Having disarmed principalities and powers, He made a public spectacle of them, triumphing over them in it.'* (Colossians 2:15)

Like a confined prisoner, the only weapon he has left is his ability to lie and deceive people. As a restrained and defeated foe, he lies to anyone who will listen.

Jesus boldly proclaimed to His disciples,

> *'I saw Satan fall like lightning from heaven. Behold, I give **you** the authority to trample on serpents and scorpions, and over all the power of the enemy, and nothing shall by any means hurt you.'* (Luke 10:18–19)

Our struggle is not with the devil as much as with the power of our flesh. As Paul describes our wrestling with flesh, he says,

> *'For the **flesh lusts against the Spirit, and the Spirit against the flesh**; and these are contrary to one another, so that you do not do the things that you wish.'* (Galatians 5:17)

Paul doesn't mention the devil in this passage, but declares that the battle is between the flesh and the Spirit.

Where does the devil come in? He comes in when we open the door to him through **uncrucified flesh**. The devil is continually looking for open doors. That is why Peter exhorts us in such a manner.

> *'Be sober, be vigilant; because your adversary the devil walks about like a roaring lion, seeking whom he may devour.'* (1 Peter 5:8)

Uncrucified Flesh

Jesus said to his disciples, *'The ruler (prince) of this world is coming, and **he has nothing in Me**'* (John 14:30). There was no place in Jesus' flesh that the devil had access to. Jesus was dead to Himself, His own agenda, His own desires.

The devil defeats Christians who live with uncrucified flesh, leaving the door open to torment and harassment. Frankly, he is looking for a place to lodge. Any area of our life will do. A friend shared with me recently how there was a certain area of her life, where she could not obtain victory. The Lord spoke to her that the devil keeps dredging things up because she's running from them. He told her to face it, because when she ran away from the problem, she opened herself to fear. When fear entered, so did hopelessness and the feelings of oppression and death. Facing ourselves and situations is the way of the Spirit. Although it appears to be painful at first, the Holy Spirit will undergird us and enable us to declare that area crucified once and for all. Ultimately our flesh has to die. It has to be crucified with Christ. Paul exhorts us to *'reckon yourselves to be dead indeed to sin, but alive to God in Christ Jesus our Lord'* (Romans 6:11).

To the Galatians he writes,

> *'And those who are Christ's **have crucified** the flesh with its passions and desires.'* (Galatians 5:24)

Paul said of himself,

> '*I have been crucified* with Christ; it is no longer I who
> live, but Christ lives in me; and the life which I now live
> in the flesh I live by faith in the Son of God, who loved
> me and gave Himself for me.'   (Galatians 2:20)

Peter is Dead to the Flesh

When Simon the sorcerer offered Peter money, he saw that
the Holy Spirit was given through the laying on of hands,
saying,

> '*Give me this power also, that anyone on whom I lay
> hands may receive the Holy Spirit.'*   (Acts 8:19)

Peter didn't respond by asking, 'How much money do
you have?'

Instead he strongly rebuked Simon saying,

> '*Your money perish with you, because you thought that
> the gift of God could be purchased with money! You
> have neither part nor portion in this matter, for your
> heart is not right in the sight of God. Repent therefore
> of this your wickedness, and pray God if* **perhaps the
> thought of your heart** *may be forgiven you. For I see
> that you are poisoned by bitterness and bound by
> iniquity.'*   (Acts 8:20–22)

There was nothing in Peter that would respond to the
sensation and temptation of money! His flesh was crucified. In fact so strong was the rebuke, that Simon
answered, '*Pray to the Lord for me, that none of the things
which you have spoken may come upon me*' (Acts 8:24).
God wants His servants so **dead** to fleshly desires that He
is the only One to Whom we respond. Many ministries
have been defiled by the love of money because they
refuse to let God crucify that area of their flesh.

What is Flesh?

Flesh can clearly be defined as **anything that is not ener-gized** by the Holy Spirit. Much activity is perpetuated by Christians that is not Holy Spirit initiated and ordained. Enormous energy in the body of Christ is wasted because believers don't take time to seek counsel from the Lord before acting on an idea that comes to mind.

> ' *"Woe to the rebellious children," says the Lord, "Who take counsel, but not of Me, and who devise plans, but not of My Spirit . . . "* ' (Isaiah 30:1)

God is a trouble saver. When He says no to a certain plan we have, it is only to spare us from expending energy which will bear little fruit.

For far too long, we in the body of Christ have tried to do God's work with man's wisdom, enthusiasm and ingenuity.

The bottom line for every believer is that God wants to rule our flesh. He wants to kill the self-will in us, including the 'I'm going to do something great for God' self-will.

The hardest message for us to hear is, 'not I, but Christ.'

> *'I have been crucified with Christ; it is no longer I who live . . . '* (Galatians 2:20)

Flesh encompasses all aspects of our old man. Paul tells us to put off the old man and put on the new man. *'That you put off, concerning your former conduct, the old man which grows corrupt according to the deceitful lusts'* (Ephesians 4:22).

> *'Do not lie to one another, since you have **put off the old man** with his deeds, and have **put on the new man** who is renewed in knowledge according to the image of Him who created him.'* (Colossians 3:9–10)

Don't be deceived into thinking this flesh will improve. It is rotten to the core. Flesh can be defined as fear, resentment, unforgiveness, selfishness, covetousness, greed, anger, fluctuating moods, sexual lusts, witchcraft, conceit, inferiority, pride. It is all self. Me, me, me.

Lord, You've Saved Me From Sin; Now Save Me From Myself

It is one thing to be saved, and quite another thing to be mature.

Part of Jesus' agony at Gethsemane had to be in accessing the Father for the strength to abstain from His willful desire to deliver Himself. He could have escaped the agony of submitting His will to death on the cross. He could have called thousands of angels to His aid. The Father would have honored His request.

Many of our prayers are to deliver ourselves, asking God to give us a quick escape from our situation, rather than asking Him to bring forth His character within us.

It is safe to say, that many of the problems we have as individuals are brought on by ourselves. Whether it is impulsive decisions, the inability to make decisions, plain disobedience, or irrational thinking, ultimately, we have no choice but to **take responsibility** for our own lives. When we do, all heaven rejoices and comes to our aid.

The most difficult problem any human being encounters is facing himself, yet that is where maturity transpires. We **all** have blind spots, and how easy it is to justify our own situation and fault the other person, not to mention envying those who seem to be in better straits.

> *'Every way of a man is right in his own eyes, but the Lord weighs the hearts.'* (Proverbs 21:2)

> *'And if one member suffers, all the members suffer with it; or if one member is honored, all the members rejoice with it.'* (1 Corinthians 12:26)

Don't Let Me Fall into the Hands of Man

When David in disobedience took a census of the number of his fighting men in Israel, the judgment of God fell.

> *'And God was displeased with this thing; therefore He struck Israel. So David said to God, "I have sinned greatly, because I have done this thing; but now, I pray, take away the iniquity of Your servant, for I have done very foolishly."'*   (1 Chronicles 21:7–8)

The Lord required that there be consequences for David's sin, and He offered him three choices.

> *'And the Lord spoke to Gad, David's seer, saying. "Go and tell David, saying, 'Thus says the Lord: "I offer you three things; choose one of them for yourself, that I may do it to you."'"'*   (1 Chronicles 21:9–10)

The Lord offered David three choices of punishment: Three years of famine, three months to be defeated by his enemies, or three days of the angel of the Lord destroying throughout the territory of Israel.

David threw himself at God's mercy, and specifically pleaded that he wouldn't fall into the hands of man. He knew man would be harsher with him than God.

> **'And David said to Gad, "I am in great distress. Please let me fall into the hand of the Lord, for His mercies are very great; but do not let me fall into the hand of man."'**   (1 Chronicles 21:13)

David not only had a wonderful understanding of God, being known as a man after God's heart, but he also had a keen understanding of the power of the flesh. He knew of God's mercy, but he knew that falling into man's hands would be without mercy.

Similarly, we see Jesus referring to the flesh of man in the same manner.

> *'Now when He was in Jerusalem at the Passover, during the feast, many believed in His name when they saw the signs which He did.* **But Jesus did not commit Himself to them, because He knew all men, and had no need that anyone should testify of man, for He knew what was in man.'** (John 2:23–25)

Flesh is Deadly

The flesh is deadly. It has no mercy. Nothing can hurt us like flesh can. That is why God warns us not to seek the praise of people and not to put confidence in the flesh of people.

> *'For they loved the praise of men more than the praise of God.'* (John 12:43)

> *'For we are the circumcision, who worship God in the Spirit, rejoice in Christ Jesus, and have* **no confidence in the flesh.'** (Philippians 3:3)

> *'It is better to trust in the Lord than to put confidence in man.'* (Psalm 118:8)

> *'The fear of man brings a snare.'* (Proverbs 29:25)

> *'In God (I will praise His word), In God I have put my trust; I will not fear.* **What can flesh do to me?'** (Psalm 56:4)

I have learned (the hard way) never to take things personally. If people praise you and hail your ministry, those same people may turn against you if you slip up, or even if they hear a rumor that you slipped up. Never take praise personally. Just realize that, by God's grace, He has used you to be a blessing. Equally, never take persecution personally. Jesus promised if they persecuted Him they will persecute you as well (John 15:20).

The safest and wisest way to live is to keep our focus on God, and desire to please Him. He will not fail us.

It seems that God has designed the human body in such a way that it is impossible to pat ourselves on the back as well as it is impossible to kick ourselves. Maybe it is because we are to do neither! We are not to coddle ourselves and lift ourselves up. But nor should we beat up on ourselves.

God doesn't exalt us or diminish us. He just reminds us that we are no more and that our life is in Him.

> *'For you died, and your life is hidden with Christ in God.'* (Colossians 3:3)

If we brag on ourselves we are in the flesh. But we are equally in the flesh if we belittle ourselves. We are not to do either. Whether we are inflated with pride, or deflated with inferiority, it is all flesh. Our identity is in Him. We live to exalt Him!

Flesh or the Devil?

We know as believers that we have authority over the devil. *'Resist the Devil and he will flee from you'* (James 4:7). We have learned not to converse with evil spirits, rather rebuke them.

But flesh is another story. For example, do you know a stubborn person? Have you ever tried to change that stubborn person's mind? Stubbornness is flesh. Flesh is a harder problem to deal with than the devil.

Rebellion says, 'I won't do it!'

Stubbornness says, 'I'll do it ... **my way!**'

Self-centeredness says, 'I want what I want, when I want it.'

It's all flesh!

Attributes of Flesh

Paul lists 17 areas of flesh in Galatians chapter 5. But let me list a few that fall within those categories.

1. Legalism

Legalism is a product of the flesh, not of the Spirit. It has a spiritual look, but it is rooted in self-righteousness.

What makes legalism so deceptive is that it is easier to adopt non-bending rules, than to listen for the heart of God in a matter. Jesus accused the Pharisees of reading Scriptures, but not realizing they spoke of Him (John 5:37).

Legalism kills. Consider divorce. Legalists tell any divorced person never to remarry, regardless of circumstances. They deafen their ears to the fact that the woman may have had her life threatened and been married to a reprobate. They are unbending and don't care what the heart of God says because they are more secure in rules than in God Himself.

2. A bad disposition

Whether it is moodiness, pouting, wearing a scowl, depression, hot-headedness, etc., all are simply a manifestation of the flesh. As Christians we are called to be Christlike, or like Christ. None of these attributes should remain in us once we have been redeemed, as they are strictly products of the flesh. It is easy to yield to a multitude of these characteristics, but the Bible exhorts us to put off that flesh and to put on the new man – Christ.

> 'That you **put off**, concerning your former conduct, the old man which grows corrupt according to the deceitful lusts, and **be renewed in the spirit of your mind**, and that you **put on** the new man which was created according to God, in true righteousness and holiness.'
>
> (Ephesians 4:22–24)

3. Self-centeredness

It is the ultimate of flesh in control. Flesh always puts self first and rarely considers the well-being of any person other than self. Sadly, self-serving, self-exalting, and self-love are so deeply ingrained in some that they never grow out of them. Although exposed to massive Bible teaching and full of knowledge, their character has remained unchanged, and is still primarily self-oriented. *'Knowledge puffs up, but love edifies'* (1 Corinthians 8:1). Those who refuse to mature are merely milk-drinkers who have refused to cooperate with the Holy Spirit by exercising their spiritual man.

> *'. . . and you have come to need milk and not solid food. For everyone who partakes only of milk is unskilled in the word of righteousness, for he is a babe. But solid food belongs to those who are of full age, that is, those who by reason of use have their senses exercised to discern both good and evil.'* (Hebrews 5:12–14)

4. Lack of discipline

When life or aspects of our life are without discipline, flesh is in control. Discipline is a decision of the will and an attribute of God. Paul said, *'But I discipline my body and bring it under subjection, lest, when I have preached to others, I myself should become disqualified'* (1 Corinthians 9:27).

5. Boasting

Boasting is flesh personified. It glorifies flesh and not God. It should be far from the lips of any saint. Boasting is carnal and is a worldly, world-loving trait. *'But "he who glories, let him glory in the Lord"'* (2 Corinthians 10:17).

> *'If anyone boast, let him boast that He understands and knows Me'* (Jeremiah 9:24)

6. Stubbornness

Unyieldedness and stubbornness are attributes of the flesh. There is nothing more difficult or impossible than to persuade a stubborn person to change his mind. A locked will is immovable and unbending. If you resist the devil, he has to flee, but the stubborn person is inflexible. Stubbornness is nothing more than flesh that refuses to submit to the Holy Spirit. A stubborn person makes idols of his own opinions, his own way, his pet doctrine, and his own ideas.

7. Idolatry and covetousness

The flesh easily yields to the desire to covet and idolize. Flesh desires what it doesn't have, and wants it as soon as possible. The best definition of lust is, **I want it now!** The Holy Spirit spoke to me the definition of idolatry. He said, 'Idolatry is whatever is foremost on your mind.'

> *'Therefore put to death your members which are on the earth: fornication, uncleanness, passion, evil desire, and **covetousness, which is idolatry**.'* (Colossians 3:5)

8. Impulsiveness

Some people are born impulsive. In the Kingdom of God, this fleshly trait has to be submitted to the Holy Spirit, or the person can easily make the wrong decisions, and quench the Holy Spirit. Most impulsive people are well-intentioned, but suffer greatly from consequences of bad decisions made on impulse. This impulsive and restless nature is a trait of the flesh that must be crucified. *'For as many as are led by the Spirit of God, these are the sons of God'* (Romans 8:14).

9. Passivity

At the other end of impulsiveness is passivity, which is flesh that refuses to respond. While passivity has an appearance of peacefulness, it is akin to laziness and procrastination. The passive person will not take his rightful place in God. He will always 'cop out' and not exert authority and strength. Many Christians with great potential have yielded their flesh to passivity. Rather than aggressively claiming and possessing the promises of the Kingdom, they choose the comfort zone of passivity, expecting nothing, and possessing nothing that God has for them. *'Woe to you who are at ease in Zion...'* (Amos 6:1).

10. Pride

There is nothing on this earth as strong, or as ugly as pride. Pride reeks of the unspoken message, 'I am at the center of my life, and I am in control.' Naturally pride is at the other end of humility. How does God look at pride?

> *'God resists the proud, but gives grace to the humble.'*
> (James 4:6)

> *'These six things the Lord hates, yes seven are an abomination to Him: A proud look...'*
> (Proverbs 6:16–17)

Because of pride, people will cheat themselves out of years of their life. Rather than apologize in a situation, admit wrongdoing, or admit their own helplessness, people will unyieldingly hold onto pride. Some have even served prison terms rather than come to grips with their own unrelenting pride.

The Bottom Line

Christians must face up to the fact that their real battle is with their flesh. The power of flesh, which is capable of opposing the Holy Spirit in all He wants to do, far exceeds the 'power' of the enemy. Jesus has already dealt a death blow to Satan! Now He desires to rule from the throne He has established at the center of our lives. All flesh must submit to His Kingship. He is Lord.

Flesh Personified

Late one afternoon I arrived at an electronics store where a tape player was being installed in my car. Upon paying the bill, the salesman, noticing the reverend on my check, asked me where I pastored. I explained that I was an evangelist. He told me that he and the other salesman standing close by were Christians. Then they began to talk about their church. One began to tell me how wonderful his pastor was and what a fine preacher he was. On and on he went in praise of his pastor, to the point of being ridiculous. In fact, he explained how, on the previous Sunday, the pastor preached so powerfully (loudly) that he couldn't even preach the second service, having lost his voice. He had to turn the service over to the assistant pastor. That didn't sound too productive to me.

The more he talked, the heavier my spirit became because no mention was made about the awesome God we serve or of His goodness. Then another lady approached us. She appeared to be in her sixties. She too, is a Christian, they exclaimed. Immediately, she started bragging about her pastor, asking me if I had ever heard of brother so and so. When I admitted that I had not, she began a lengthy spiel about the fact that her pastor was beyond wonderful, and that he is not only a marvelous preacher, but an awesome businessman. 'Because of his abilities,' she explained to me, 'we have 6000 members and absolutely no division in our church.' She continued to gloat about this man she had on a pedestal, while her expressions exuded self-righteousness. Of course she had no interest in my ministry, and directed no questions to me, since her pastor was the ultimate.

I departed that place of business sickened from the 'flesh personified' conversation. Four Christians were conversing, yet nothing was mentioned about the Lord.

Although twice, when someone took a breath I forced in the words, 'The Lord is so good.' No one acknowledged what I said.

When people are mesmerized by the man of God, rather than God, it borders on idolatry. It certainly quenches the spirit and doesn't advance the Gospel. The King of kings and Lord of lords is not exalted, rather Reverend Wonderful is extolled.

Those leaders who cause people to elevate them rather than insist that all focus be put on God, are nothing more than manipulators and controllers. They have used their position and influence to eclipse God and leave people with a high impression of themselves.

Another pastor we know of has a thriving church, largely due to adding members from other churches splitting off. I have seen numerous people join this church, and without exception, they all have lost their zeal and hunger for the Lord and become totally consumed in working for that church. When they speak of this pastor it is nothing but adulation for this man, to the point of being obnoxious.

He will immediately grant permission to all who want to start a ministry of almost any sort, and usually allows them to use a portion of the church facilities for it. We are supposed to seek God on these matters. Doesn't the Holy Spirit have a say if a specific type of ministry is put in motion?

Listening to this man is like listening to a personality who is skilled in communication, but deficient (if not devoid) of the anointing. Yet people do not seem troubled that their vision has been sucked out of them. The only vision they have is that this pastor is a wonderful man.

Mixing Flesh and Spirit

There is no greater contrast in the earth than that of flesh and Spirit.

Christians carry a responsibility before God to let their

light shine before men (Matthew 5:16). What confuses the unbeliever and the baby Christian is when those, who are supposedly mature in the Lord, don't live a life of consistency in the Holy Spirit. When they see a seasoned Christian act with impropriety, foolishness, or even malicious gossip, it confuses the new believer. The same way a parent has the responsibility of not exhibiting ugly conduct in front of a small child, so too, the Christian has a responsibility to walk in the Spirit at all times.

There is a responsibility we have as Christians to live in Christ. Many baby Christians have been permanently disabled because they have beheld a 'spiritual' person stand before people and function in the gifts of the Spirit. Yet, a day later, they see that same person conduct himself in a fleshly manner or with unrighteous talk or conduct. In that baby Christian's mind, this causes confusion, because he is unable to distinguish between the person's gift and His character. Seeing fleshly behavior either confuses the baby Christian, thinking that it doesn't matter to God to act unrighteously, or convinces him he doesn't want to serve a God who uses such unrighteous people.

> *'Dead flies putrefy the perfumer's ointment, and cause it to give off a foul odor; so does a **little** folly to one respected for wisdom and honor.'* (Ecclesiastes 10:1)

Turned into Another Man

A graphic Scripture explains how Saul briefly turned into another man, when he was under the anointing, to prophesy. *'Then the Spirit of the Lord will come upon you, and you will prophesy with them and be **turned into another man**'* (1 Samuel 10:6).

It is easy to be spiritual when one is under the anointing, or when one is in the presence of those who are moving with the anointing.

However, God's concern is not what we are when we minister under the anointing, but that we are transformed permanently into 'another man', that is, into the image and character of Christ.

God's Goal

God's goal for each of us is maturity. He works with us to bring us to the fullness of His likeness.

> *'That we should no longer be children, tossed to and fro and carried about with every wind of doctrine, by the trickery of men, in the cunning craftiness of deceitful plotting, but, speaking the truth in love, **may grow in all things** unto Him who is the head – Christ.'*
>
> (Ephesians 4:14–15)

- It's not what you've done, it's what you've become.

Chapter 3

Jezebel – The Ultimate of Flesh in Control

There is no place that the flesh rules more ruthlessly than through the Jezebel personality.

The commonly used term, Jezebel, was in actuality the name of the wicked Queen Jezebel, the wife of King Ahab, in the Old Testament. She was the daughter of a Sidonian king who made a trade agreement with Israel's King Ahab. Part of the agreement included Jezebel, the daughter. Because of the control she exercised and the tactics she used to exert illegitimate and wicked control over people, her name has become synonymous with the spirit of control.

Jezebel is a product of the flesh that opens the door to an evil spirit. Paul called witchcraft a work of the flesh (Galatians 5:20). It is behavior that operates through a person to control by the use of manipulative, domineering and intimidating tactics. Although not restricted to either sex, it often is acknowledged to be more prevalent in women; but there is no question that it functions just as proficiently through men.

Where it functions through women, the Jezebel spirit seems to serve as Satan's answer to a male-dominated world, to give a false protection in a world where a woman seemingly never gets her rights, and the protective love of a father and a husband. Out of the lack of love, she rebels against the whole unloving system, and becomes just like it. The controlled becomes the controller; the oppressed becomes the oppressor.

Whether male or female, controllers are almost always motivated out of insecurity.

Jezebel Was Religious

Probably most deceiving to many is that Jezebel is religious, and does religious things. She was the daughter of Ethbaal, meaning 'with Baal'. She converted her husband Ahab to follow Baal. Ahab married her against God's command.

The name, Jezebel, specifically means without dwelling or habitation. This is true of her nature; she is independent; she co-habits with no one. Her name can also be defined as unmarried, or uncommitted. She is committed to no one except her own self-will. A true explanation of Jezebel can clearly be described as the worship of self-will.

The worship of Baal was an idolatrous religion, worshiping false gods – the work of one's hands and included child sacrifice, perverted heterosexual relationships and homosexual activity.

Elijah called for the prophets, who ate at Jezebel's table, to come forth.

> *'Now therefore, send and gather all Israel to me on Mount Carmel, the four hundred and fifty prophets of Baal, and the four hundred prophets of Asherah, who eat at Jezebel's table.'* (1 Kings 18:19)

He called the children of Israel together along with the prophets of Baal to Mount Carmel, challenging the prophets of Baal to call on their God to consume the sacrifice. When they failed, he rebuilt the altar and called upon the Lord. When the fire of God fell, the Israelites turned back to God.

> *'Now when all the people saw it, they fell on their faces: and they said, "The Lord, He is God! The Lord, He is God!" '* (1 Kings 18:39)

Then he commanded that the prophets of Baal be executed.

> *'And Elijah said to them, "Seize the prophets of Baal! Do not let one of them escape!" So they seized them; and Elijah brought them down to the Brook Kishon and executed them there.'* (1 Kings 18:40)

The clear battle with the Jezebel spirit is over **people**. That spirit desires to rule and control the people of God. If we are not people of decision, we will fall under the spell of the Jezebel spirit.

To describe her agenda would be to say she exalts position over character.

She was a supporter of, and heavily influential in, religious organization as well as politics. While Jezebel is religious, she wields her false power against the true prophetic flow of God. She hates the prophets and all prophetic ministry.

Specifically, she hates repentance, humility, and intercessory prayer, because they destroy her stronghold of stubbornness, pride and fervency for the mind of God.

When Elijah had killed all the prophets of Baal, Ahab abdicated his authority to Jezebel, telling her what Elijah had done.

> *'And Ahab told Jezebel all that Elijah had done, also how he had executed all the prophets with the sword.'* (1 Kings 19:1)

Jezebel was furious.

> *'Then Jezebel sent a messenger unto Elijah, saying "So let the gods do to me, and more also, if I do not make*

your life as the life of one of them by tomorrow about this time."' (1 Kings 19:2)

Why Did Elijah Run?

The fact that Elijah was so powerful in God, yet he ran for his life from one woman, is perplexing.

> *'And when he saw that, he arose and ran for his life, and went to Beer-sheba, which belongs to Judah, and left his servant there. But he himself went a day's journey into the wilderness, and came and sat down under a broom tree. And he prayed that he might die, and said, "It is enough! Now, Lord, take my life, for I am no better than my fathers!"'* (1 Kings 19:3–4)

Some of the greatest effectiveness of the Jezebel spirit is that of intimidation. Her threats carried such a vengeance, that Elijah responded to fear, instead of God.

Jezebels love to project a sense of power that they do not have. It is based on fear and intimidation, in order to cloud the minds of those they desire to oppress.

How frequently that spirit tries to wield influence.

In the church – 'If you take this action, we will withhold our tithe.' Or, 'Submit to me, or you won't have a spiritual covering.'

In the family – 'If you don't see it my way, you can sleep in another bed.' Or, 'I'll leave, and take the kids with me.'

In a business – 'You can forget about a promotion.' Or, 'I'll sue this company until you go out of business.'

These are all improper channels, a use of illegitimate power and authority, a projection of power that is not **ours** to use.

This by no means insinuates that a person shouldn't stand up for himself, but that it should be done through proper channels. Manipulating, intimidating and dominating another human being are blatant uses of control, and illegitimate authority.

Elijah was temporarily influenced by fear, which caused him to be bound by discouragement, despair and paralyzed by this projected 'power'. But God delivered him.

Jezebel was so intimidating that, when God confronted Elijah, his words were,

> *'I have been very zealous for the Lord God of hosts; for the children of Israel have forsaken Your covenant, torn down Your altars, and killed Your prophets with the sword. **I alone am left.**'* (1 Kings 19:10)

The spirit of intimidation was so strong that it was projected in his mind there was not another person left who was devoted to God. That spirit wants you to feel abandoned, to surrender to hopelessness. It desires to paralyze the prophetic flow of God.

However, it is clear that Elijah had surrendered to self-pity. Self-pity is clearly a conscious resignation and surrendering to the victim mentality. When you see yourself as a victim, you literally enter into sin with Jezebel, because you are not resisting her. For example, in our society, those who do not stand up against the pro-abortion philosophy and other liberal and worldly standards, are in effect entering into sin with her. The way to stand against that life-style and spirit is through prayer, commitment to truth, and a willingness to confront lies.

God quickly clarified Elijah's perspective.

> *'Yet I have reserved seven thousand in Israel, **all** whose knees have not bowed to Baal, and **every mouth** that has not kissed him.'* (1 Kings 19:18)

She Gets What She Wants

There is something so stubborn, so mean-spirited, so jealous, and so determined, in a Jezebel. Seemingly nothing will stop her from getting what she wants.

When Naboth refused to sell Ahab his vineyard, Jezebel immediately took things into her own hands.

> *'So Ahab went into his house sullen and displeased because of the word which Naboth the Jezreelite had spoken to him; for he had said, "I will not give thee the inheritance of my fathers." And he lay down on his bed, and turned away his face, and would eat no food.*
>
> *But Jezebel his wife came to him, and said unto him, "Why is your spirit so sullen that you eat no food?" And he said to her, "Because I spoke to Naboth the Jezreelite, and said to him, 'Give me your vineyard for money; or else, if it pleases you, I will give you another vineyard for it.' And he answered, 'I will not give you my vineyard.' "*
>
> *Then Jezebel his wife said to him, "You now exercise authority over Israel! Arise, eat food, and let your heart be cheerful;* **I will give you** *the vineyard of Naboth the Jezreelite." '* (1 Kings 21:4–7)

Quickly Jezebel appointed herself to do what her husband wasn't 'king enough' to do.

A Jezebel has absolutely no regard for godly authority. Her spirit is in exact contrast to the will of God.

Her will has become god. Her will must be accomplished, regardless of the consequences. No price is too great; no life is too precious to get her will manifested. Her theology is that the end justifies the means – condoning sin, and even murder, to accomplish her wishes.

Basically, the spirit of Jezebel has no conscience. Those under its control have hardened their hearts and their consciences are seared. Their will is king and they are supreme.

Illegitimate Authority

The most dastardly expression of a Jezebel spirit is the way she usurps authority that is not her own.

She began by writing letters in Ahab's name.

> *'And she wrote letters in Ahab's name, sealed them with*
> *his seal, and sent the letters to the elders and the nobles*
> *who were dwelling in the city with Naboth. She wrote in*
> *the letters, saying, "Proclaim a fast, and seat Naboth*
> *with high honor among the people; and seat two men,*
> *scoundrels, before him to bear witness against him,*
> *saying, 'You have blasphemed God and the king.' Then*
> *take him out, and stone him, that he may die."'*

(1 Kings 21:8–10)

Not only did she steal authority, she manipulated those in leadership. She used lies and distortions, and even used a religious term, fasting, and a religious occasion to bring her wickedness to pass.

She Always Gets Others to do Her Dirty Work

This is an extremely predictable 'method' of a Jezebel. She uses others to do her dirty work. Commonly, a Jezebel will stir innocent people up until their emotions get out of control, then will stand passively by, saying, 'What did I do wrong?' Most assuredly, she will never take any blame.

The elders and nobles of Naboth's city followed her revolting command.

> *'So the men of his city, the elders and the nobles who*
> *were the inhabitants of his city, did as Jezebel had sent*
> *to them, as it was written in the letters which she had*
> *sent to them. They proclaimed a fast, and seated*
> *Naboth with high honor among the people. And two*
> *men, scoundrels came in and sat before him; and the*
> *scoundrels witnessed against him, against Naboth, in*
> *the presence of the people, saying, "Naboth has blas-*
> *phemed God and the king!" Then they took him outside*
> *the city and stoned him with stones, so that he died.'*

(1 Kings 21:11–13)

The saddest aspect is the way the Jezebel spirit destroys the fruitfulness of others. Ahab, acting like a spoiled child, wanted the vineyard for his selfish convenience. Refusing to have the backbone to stand up to the spirit of control, he relinquished his authority into the hands of his wife and an innocent man was killed. Naboth's fruitfulness ended.

Naboth simply felt he could not give up the inheritance of his fathers to the king for such a selfish reason. The Jezebel spirit desires that righteous people forsake their convictions in order for it to do its religious work.

What About Ahab?

Ahab was spineless. He quickly abdicated his authority to his wife. Even God said of Ahab,

> *'But there was no one like Ahab who sold himself to do wickedness in the sight of the Lord, because Jezebel his wife **stirred him up**. And he behaved very abominably in following idols, according to all that the Amorites had done, whom the Lord had cast out before the children of Israel.'* (1 Kings 21:25–26)

While Jezebel was quick to take authority that didn't belong to her, Ahab was **just as guilty**, by surrendering his rightful authority.

There is nothing more nauseating than a spineless person; specifically a person who is in a position of authority, such as a husband, a pastor, or an elected politician, who gives his authority away in order to please someone, while compromising his own beliefs and convictions.

Many fit into the Ahab category today, because they are people pleasers, and won't stand up to the Jezebel spirit.

Those who serve Jezebel die first. Ahab's life was cut short.

> *'Notwithstanding I have a few things against you, because you tolerate the woman Jezebel...'*
>
> (Revelation 2:20 KJV)

How pleased God would have been if Ahab had stood up to the controlling and manipulative spirit of Jezebel. But instead, he let her walk all over him, usurping his position.

While many men are guilty of dominating their wives and families, other men cower down to the spirit of control, fearing an interruption of their sex life, verbal abuse, etc. which are illegitimate tools a woman may use to get her way.

In other situations, people surrender to a controlling, dominating, egotistic male, not standing up to that controlling spirit and personality.

She Surrounded Herself with Eunuchs

It is most interesting that Jezebel had eunuchs at her side. They were men she had emasculated of their manhood and authority.

It was a welcome vindication to them no doubt when they were able to throw her down at the command of Jehu.

Jehu was an instrument God could use. The name Jehu means **Jehovah is He**. As the newly anointed king of Israel (2 Kings 9:6), he was given a clear command through the prophet of God.

> *'You shall strike down the house of Ahab your master, that I may avenge the blood of My servants the prophets, and the blood of all the servants of the Lord, at the hand of Jezebel.'* (2 Kings 9:7)

The mistake many make when dealing with a person with a Jezebel spirit is that of being too easy on it.

Just as Jehu commanded her to be thrown down, we must be aggressive and not tolerate her.

When the horseman met Jehu coming into the city, he asked him, *'Thus says the king, "Is it peace?"'* (2 Kings 9:18).

Jehu said, *'What have you to do with peace? Turn around and follow me'* (2 Kings 9:18). He said the same thing to the second horseman that approached him.

Furiously Determined

It was reported to the king that *'the driving is like the driving of Jehu the son of Nimshi, for he drives furiously!'* (2 Kings 9:20).

Those who deal with the spirit of Jezebel must be without compromise, non-relenting, and aggressive against it. There can be no tolerance for it. You must be an aggressive 'driver'. As Jehu, we must be furiously determined.

Notice his statement.

King Joram asks Jehu, *'Is it peace, Jehu?'* (2 Kings 9:22).

Jehu answered,

> *'What peace, as long as the harlotries of your mother Jezebel and her witchcraft are so many?'*
>
> (2 Kings 9:22)

There is no question that there is no room for compromise in him. To confront this spirit we must be ruthless toward it, showing no mercy, no sympathy toward it and its behavior. We must realize that we are dealing with an evil spirit, and although we must be compassionate to the person in its clutches, we must deal a death blow to the evil spirit.

Next Jehu kills King Jehoram and King Ahaziah and then went to confront Jezebel.

> *'Now when Jehu had come to Jezreel, Jezebel heard of it; and she put paint on her eyes and adorned her head,*

and looked through a window. Then, as Jehu entered at the gate, she said, "Is it peace, Zimri, murderer of your master?"' (2 Kings 9:30–31)

She was still using her seductive tactics to influence him.

Throw Her Down!

Jehu must have made heaven applaud as he looked up at the window, speaking with great authority, *'**"Who is on my side? Who?"** So two or three eunuchs looked out at him'* (2 Kings 9:32).

He immediately commanded those eunuchs to throw her down. There is such significance in this. Those who had been castrated by her and humiliated and rendered powerless, **became instruments in her destruction**. Sweet vindication.

'Then he said, "Throw her down." So they threw her down, and some of her blood spattered on the wall and on the horses; and he trampled her underfoot.'
(2 Kings 9:33)

Those who have been victims of this treacherous spirit must rise up in the power of God and be ruthless against it. Let God use you to be an instrument in throwing her down. Stop compromising with that spirit and cling to the purpose of God. Too many lack victory because they live in false peace where the spirit of Jezebel is concerned. This is a day when we must live without compromise and never surrender to fear.

It is interesting to note how the word of the Lord had come to pass where Jezebel's life was concerned.

'And concerning Jezebel the Lord also spoke, saying, "The dogs shall eat Jezebel by the wall of Jezreel."'
(1 Kings 21:23)

After the eunuchs threw her down, Jehu used his horse to trample her underfoot. When they went to bury her, they found no more of her than her skull, her feet, and the palms of her hands. Rather than the dignity of a grave, her corpse became as refuse on the surface of the field (2 Kings 9:35–37).

The name Jezreel means God soweth. God sowed a disaster plan against her and her wickedness.

God desires to bring eternal judgment to the spirit of Jezebel. Its influence in the church must end. God is raising up those who will be militant against that spirit. Not only by becoming unyielding and aggressive against it, but by living in full repentance and walking in total humility, and loving truth more than popularity and reputation.

The Jezebel Spirit Will Be Judged

The Jezebel spirit destroys families, churches, businesses and relationships. It destroys lives. Therefore, God hates it and will bring judgment upon it.

However, something that has always troubled me is the way that those who yield to the Jezebel spirit seem to get away with it.

First of all, God is merciful, and gives the person time to repent.

> *'Nevertheless I have a few things against you, because you allow that woman Jezebel, who calls herself a prophetess, to teach and seduce My servants to commit sexual immorality and eat things sacrificed to idols. And **I gave her time to repent** of her sexual immorality, and she did not repent.'* (Revelation 2:20–21)

God is so merciful and always reaches out to bring the person to repentance before judgment comes.

Secondly, God waits for someone to stand up to her – to confront her. Many succumb to the Ahab spirit and simply turn their head from her tactics. They reason that, after all she is religious, and works hard in the church. The greatest weakness among leaders is the fear of confrontation. They want peace without paying the price of confronting the manipulation and controlling tactics of the Jezebel spirit.

Honestly, in my years of ministry, I have rarely seen a true Jezebel delivered. Sometimes he becomes temporarily remorseful, but soon he'll go back to his controlling tactics. The learned behavior is deeply rooted, and the person enjoys the taste of power (although distorted) and must fervently desire deliverance.

The Jezebel Spirit Purposes to Destroy the Prophetic

The devil hates the prophetic flow of God, because the prophetic ministry demands repentance, and cuts away evil without compromise. The prophet always speaks against her. Additionally the prophetic words come with creative power, which renders the enemy helpless.

There is such significance in the fact that Jezebel wanted to destroy Elijah. That spirit hates the prophetic, non-compromising voice. It cannot accomplish its agenda with a prophet around.

The same spirit operated through Herodias, after John the Baptist confronted King Herod.

> '*For Herod himself had sent and laid hold of John, and bound him in prison for the sake of Herodias, his brother Philip's wife; for he had married her. For John had said to Herod, "It is not lawful for you to have your brother's wife."* **Therefore, Herodias held it against him and wanted to kill him, but she could not.** *For Herod feared John, knowing that he was a just and holy man, and he protected him. And when he heard him, he did many things, and heard him gladly.*'
> (Mark 6:17–20)

The Jezebel spirit is strong and seeks what it wants, waiting for an opportunity. No wonder the Bible warns us to give no place to the devil (Ephesians 4:27).

> *'Then an opportune day came when Herod on his birthday gave a feast for his nobles, the high officers, and the chief men of Galilee. And when Herodias' daughter herself came in and danced, and pleased Herod and those who sat with him, the king said to the young girl, "Ask me whatever you want, and I will give it to you." He also swore to her, "Whatever you ask me, I will give you, up to half my kingdom." '*

> ***'So she went out and said to her mother, "What shall I ask?" And she said, "The head of John the Baptist."*** *Immediately she came in with haste to the king and asked, saying, "I want you to give me at once the head of John the Baptist on a platter." And the king was exceedingly sorry; yet, because of the oaths and because of those who sat with him, he did not want to refuse her. And immediately the king sent an executioner and commanded his head to be brought. And he went and beheaded him in prison, brought his head on a platter, and gave it to the girl; and the girl gave it to her mother.'* (Mark 6:21–28)

Again, this Jezebel spirit typically gets someone else to do its dirty work. She couldn't receive correction and seek repentance, therefore she had to destroy the one who spoke truth.

This same spirit that desired to destroy Elijah was clearly responsible for cutting off the head of John the Baptist. The spirit of Jezebel hates the prophet, because the prophetic voice demands repentance and surrendering of the self-will. The prophet calls people to the cross. Jezebel hates the cross.

God is exposing and judging the spirit of Jezebel in the church. Hallelujah.

Comparing Elijah and Jezebel

Elijah demands repentance.	Jezebel hates repentance.
Elijah demands righteousness.	Jezebel opposes righteousness.
Elijah speaks freedom.	Jezebel desires control.
Elijah demands humility.	Jezebel appeals to pride.
Elijah speaks God's ways.	Jezebel uses deceit and systems of witchcraft.

Defeating Jezebel – Disdain for All She Represents

What terrifies and cripples the power of darkness more than anything else is when believers surrender totally to the person and nature of Christ. To be Christlike is to wield a powerful weapon against the enemy, because after all, the Jezebel spirit is specifically opposed to the nature of Christ.

> *'But I have this against you, that you tolerate the woman Jezebel, who calls herself a prophetess, and she teaches and **leads My bondservants astray**, so that they **commit acts of immorality** and eat things sacrificed to idols.'* (Revelation 2:20 KJV)

There must be consistency in our lives as believers to have disdain and intolerance for all types of the influence of Jezebel. For example, many times we rejoice and worship before the Lord in church, and yet come home later and watch immoral entertainment on television. When we tolerate the influence of the spirit of Jezebel in our private lives, we give it inroads to the sanctuary of our life. This behavior doesn't fool God, and being tolerant of Jezebel, we greatly hinder the power and effectiveness of God through us.

Jesus said, *'The ruler* (prince) *of this world is coming, and he has **nothing in Me**'* (John 14:30).

The bottom line is we must equip ourselves with a new resolve to war against Jezebel. Rather than sulking in condemnation of sins we've so easily given into, we need to war aggressively against that spirit and shake off all of her influence in our lives.

Pornography

The spirit of Jezebel in the world systems is obvious. Her spirit is preeminent throughout Hollywood. She runs unchallenged through the entertainment and fashion industry. Through technological advances, multitudes have easy access to the flood of filth that flows forth into the rebellious and carnal minds which have been structured into the devil's stronghold. Liberal philosophers in the universities are strongly under her influence, shaping the minds of the young. She speaks loudly through the feminist movement, is the cruel motivator of the pro-abortion thrust, and probably most effectively through the pornographic industry.

Many leaders with mighty anointings have been seduced by this spirit through the use of pornography.

It renders the addicted one helpless to walk in victory and he is laden with guilt and shame instead. Although the pornography addict may have a totally secret indulgence, it keeps him helpless, powerless, and ineffective. *'What peace as long as the harlotries of your mother Jezebel and her witchcraft are so many?'* (2 Kings 9:22).

Just as the eunuchs were robbed of all masculinity, so those who have been tolerant and sympathetic to her nature have become spiritual eunuchs. When they pray, it is more as a eunuch robbed of all masculinity, instead of a powerful, authority-filled believer.

Prayer

(Next to our being Christlike), there is nothing that the Jezebel spirit fears more than prayer. Real prayer, is simply praying what is on the mind of God. Strategic prayer is coming into alignment with God's thoughts and praying specifically therein.

Many are bound to praying their own agenda. There is no power in that. True intercessory prayer is praying God's agenda. It throws a wrecking ball on the strategies of Jezebel, and extracts her influence from the souls of men. It stirs people to repentance, causing her to lose her influence. Intercessory prayer turns people's hearts away from immorality, bringing true repentance and godliness. True fervent intercessory prayer causes hearts to change from pride and loftiness to repentance and humility. Nothing brings a greater death blow to the spirit of Jezebel.

She no doubt fears most the spoken word of God, as it comes forth with creative power.

Prayer

Father forgive us for being tolerant of the Jezebel spirit. Open our eyes to all her influence and tactics. We bind the stronghold she has on the minds of those in our lives, church, and community, and we release the Spirit of God to expose all her works. We pull down every stronghold and fortress this spirit has built up in the area in which we live. We choose to humble ourselves and walk before you with purity of heart and mind, and a submissive spirit. In Jesus' Name.

Chapter 4

Jezebel in Action

The following three examples are everyday life situations which graphically reveal many of the characteristics of a Jezebel spirit. Many who have been victimized by those infected with this spirit, will recognize these familiar characteristics.

Office Worker

A friend of mine, who is a business executive, hired a nice appearing young woman as an office assistant. The first few days of her performance seemed fine. But it wasn't long before he noticed some strange behavior.

One of the first unusual tactics he observed was of her hiding important documents on his desk, then later in the day, being the 'hero' and finding the missing item.

When she was assigned to do anything, she would always exaggerate her accomplishments. If, for example, she was to make ten calls to hard-to-reach clients, she would make an announcement later in the day that the task was done. However, it became apparent soon after, that although she had tried to reach the ten, she had been successful in only one. This is a common characteristic of the Jezebel spirit. Jezebel types live in a world of **distortion and lies**, projecting everything, even the smallest actions, to look grandiose. Equally as common in this world of distortions is to exaggerate everything – especially their accomplishments.

She would also take credit underhandedly for tasks that other office workers had completed. This was only discovered later, because she so intimidated the other workers that they were afraid to complain. Her overpowering spirit implied and projected that she had a special relationship with her boss. She did this to wield power over the others.

One way she would exert her weird sense of power over the other workers would be to load them down with tasks just before quitting time. Again, the boss didn't find this out until later, as the other employees were too intimidated to speak up.

The longer she worked for him the more obvious it became that she would go to great lengths to make herself look big. Along with this, she always wanted instant praise and gratification for anything she did. As is typical of a Jezebel she would complain that she wasn't appreciated enough.

She was also a chronic liar, which is usually characteristic of Jezebel spirits. They can look you in the eye and be extremely persuasive as they lie. Jezebels are great liars! They are convincing! They know how to turn on charm, and they know just as quickly how to stab you in the back. Their main objective is control and power, in order to get what they want.

This young lady was consumed with greed. Yet the greed was disguised in syrupy sweetness and dramatic enthusiasm for the person she was trying to influence in her favor.

Finally this executive fired her for insubordination. She declared to him one day that she was leaving early. (She frequently came in late, as if she were an exception to any rules that others were required to abide by.) He insisted that she was needed until five o'clock. When she left anyway, screaming as she went out the door, she was terminated. The following Monday, she tried to return to work as if nothing had happened. So separated from reality, she was shocked that she no longer had a job there.

This young lady, as is characteristic of many Jezebels, had no concept of reality.

She had her lawyer write my executive friend to inform him that he was being sued for five million dollars. A week or so after she had the lawyer send the vindictive letter, she called to wish her former employer a happy birthday. The tone of her voice was as if nothing had transpired. Days later, more accusations were made. She accused this committed Christian man of cussing at her, which was simply a blatant lie. Although the case was eventually dropped, extreme exaggerated lying charges were made – and yet frequently she would make a cheerful call to him as if nothing had happened.

The three most prominent characteristics he noticed in this woman were greed, manipulation, and lying.

I asked him what he thought was the root of her intense struggle for power and control. He said that, through conversations during the months she had worked for him, she had shared with him that she was the youngest of seven girls in her family and had never been disciplined by her parents. **Children who are not disciplined often learn to manipulate**.

At a point near the end of her employment, he learned of another situation. This woman had a small water leak in the apartment she shared with her husband. As my friend observed, a person with a Jezebel spirit, takes ten ounces of power and makes it seem like two thousand pounds. **Jezebels know how to project the illusion of power when they have none**. He was appalled by the extreme anger and threats she made as she called her apartment manager from work. When he heard her make the call, the reality of her dangerous personality finally hit him, and he rightly thought, 'I'm next.'

This woman also had a major ability to generate hype. As is characteristic of the devil himself, she always strongly overplayed her hand.

Her charm was one of her mightiest weapons. She was an attractive person and knew how to turn on extreme sweetness. But as always with these spirits, that sweetness can quickly turn to a gargantuan sourness if the one she is trying to sweeten doesn't yield.

Remember Potiphar's wife? She tried to sweeten Joseph with her charms. When he refused, the same charm turned into bitterness and she cruelly accused an innocent and righteous Joseph of attempted rape (Genesis 39).

Common characteristics:
- Overemphasis of their importance
- Extreme exaggeration
- Greed
- Extremely convincing at lying
- Projecting the illusion of power
- Living in a world of distortion
- Switching from charm to killer instinct

A Doctor

Another friend of mine, who is a doctor of a specific specialty, had practised for over twenty years when a young woman, nearing the end of her medical school training approached him for a position in his practice.

Upon meeting her, he was impressed by the way she came across as helpful and very humble and teachable. He also noted that her attitude was extremely sympathetic, as she emphasized understanding when he expressed some apprehension that her joining him in the business may not work out. She intimated it would not be a problem.

However, he began to feel alarmed when, at a medical convention, she was listening to a conversation between him and a computer salesman. The salesman mentioned hiring a couple of high school girls to do some typing for him. When this woman overheard this, she butted into the conversation, and with an angry tone, said 'Why not hire a couple of guys?' (as if hiring girls was condescending).

My doctor friend was upset by this intrusion and her seemingly hostile attitude, so he began to express some dismay about their proceeding relationship.

When he approached her about this she let him know that her husband, who was an attorney, had already secured employment in the doctor's city. This is typical of Jezebels, namely **presumption** and **pushiness**. Although there was never a settled agreement, she moved in presumption and 'encouraged' her husband, who had a passive nature, to go ahead and seek employment.

With this knowledge, the doctor, not totally feeling right about it, agreed to let her come on staff, since her husband was already relocating. He felt he just couldn't say no at this point, although the woman and her manipulated husband had no right to have proceeded without an official working agreement.

Upon agreeing to let her come on staff, the doctor began to sense a constant **undermining**. In sometimes subtle, and other times not so subtle ways, she began to challenge every decision he made. In daily morning meetings, for example, she would make statements such as, 'I had trouble with the way you handled that client yesterday.' **Undermining** is so typical of a Jezebel spirit. That spirit rebels against all authority and tries to illegitimately put itself in the position of authority. The doctor many times, tried to pass this off, but kept thinking to himself, 'I'm the one who hired her, and I'm the one who's been in practice for twenty years. Who is she to be challenging me?'

Soon she began making continual demands for more backing of her work and more authority. In fact, she constantly asked for more authority, as if she were the owner of the medical practice.

Within one year, the practice went through seven employees, although the doctor had never had problems of this nature in the past. This woman would correct every employee about something in a way which greatly upset them. Then my friend would try to encourage the employee to shake it off, but one by one each employee would resign.

Later, employees who were **intimidated and fearful** of her told him how she would demand they do procedures a certain way. They would express that he had told them a specific way to do it. She would always say, 'That's alright, do it my way and I'll talk to Dr X about it.' Often employees were upset and crying but they didn't feel they could approach him, because she made them think the two of them were in total agreement.

She would also make subtle derogatory remarks about his wife and son, but it wasn't until much later he realized what was going on. Simply, she was **sowing seeds of discord**, to try to damage his family. He remembers, as he looks back, that every time he would be involved in conversation with her he would feel so dirty and polluted.

For months she would exercise her bounds of authority, as a rebellious child challenging a parent to see how much he could get away with.

Over the months he observed her with clients. She would speak highly of clients who never questioned her, but of those who would intimidate her in any way, she would speak vile things about them after they left. If people didn't cater to her, or if they ever questioned her, she hated them. This is so typical of a Jezebel. That spirit is rooted in **pride**. That is why you will **never** hear one admit wrong doing in any way. It is **always the other person's fault**. The stronghold of pride is so established in one with a Jezebel spirit, that the closest you will ever hear to an apology, is 'I'm sorry you got your feelings hurt.'

On many occasions, he would be in conversation with her and catch himself confiding in her and giving her information that was none of her business. This also is so typical of a Jezebel spirit. The person seems to have a power that makes you want to offer information. This is the work of a Jezebel spirit, namely to **extract information she can later use as ammunition against you**, if your relationship ever ceases.

She would at times work extra long hours and then expect him to work them equally. He owned the medical practice, yet would be made to feel guilty for going home.

She claimed in an article she wrote for a professional women's magazine, that she got where she was by 'herself' – no one else. She had no mentor.

When a Jezebel loses control, the same 'love and devotion' turn into hate and destruction. The love and loyalty seemingly expressed were with an evil and twisted motive for power and gain.

When he finally caught her in an act of total insubordination and fired her, she immediately sought to destroy his reputation. She approached numerous doctors, not only in that city, but in the surrounding counties. As is typical of Jezebel, she seemed to stop at nothing. Once a Jezebel loses her grip – look out! It's the same spirit that wanted Elijah's life destroyed. With every case she pleaded to the listeners how she was a victim, and distorted facts, using things he had confided in her, against him. Several colleagues, wouldn't listen to her because her stories didn't match the character of the man they knew. But in this doctor's words, 'She was hell-bent to destroy me.' Everything he ever said to her, he told me, came back to haunt him.

In her path of destruction she attempted to steal as many clients and staff as possible. Two naive students did follow her. Jezebels can be convincing.

This doctor later found out (too late) that she had a history of always hating her superiors. She was raised by a father whom she could never please, and feeling oppressed, she became the oppressor. She had abandoned her former career before medical school because of a superior who supposedly had 'mistreated and abused' her. She wasn't abused, but rather was under the authority of a superior who wouldn't put up with her manipulation and insubordination. Naturally, being a Jezebel, she would never admit that.

Common characteristics:

- Pride
- Presumption
- Pushiness
- Inability to admit wrong
- Insubordination
- Rebellion
- Sower of seeds of discord
- Hate (for those who question her)
- Intimidation
- Distortion

College Student

A friend of mine, a graduate student, began to date an attractive young woman. Their relationship was going along smoothly for the first few weeks. She loved to invite him over for meals and went out of her way to do nice things for him. Never had he been in a relationship where he had been treated so kindly and with such thoughtfulness.

However, a few weeks into the relationship, things changed. For example, one day he suggested he accompany her by car from her apartment to a local gas station two miles away so she could have a tire checked. But on the day that they had this casual commitment, he was approached by a few of his friends to play a game of basketball. When he suggested to her that rather than taking the five-minute run to the gas station with her, he would instead be involved in a basketball game, she gave him a hurt and hateful look. She wouldn't speak to him for hours. When finally he insisted on finding out why she was so upset, she began to make vile accusations against him, saying that he was uncaring and heartless. He couldn't believe what he was hearing as she flew into a jealous rage over his simple desire to shoot a few baskets.

The bottom line is control. Those who have this possessive, Jezebel love, want you one-hundred percent to themselves. Ninety-five percent is not enough. Anyone other than he or she who requires your time is an enemy, and you become the enemy for not wanting to submit **all** your time to her or him.

He found out months later that, from the beginning, she had lied about herself and made extreme exaggerations about past accomplishments and present abilities.

She would interview him about special qualities he liked in the opposite sex, then she would **become** that person. She would make up lies about herself to make him believe that she was the person of his dreams.

He was amazed at her preoccupation with herself; her selfish actions and her self-centered nature. She would go to any lengths in lying and exaggerating, to make herself look good.

She knew how to garner sympathy. She knew how to cry at the drop of a hat and fool almost anyone.

She was an excessive bragger. To hear of her family and the history of her family, you would think you were hearing of the highest royalty. She would continually compliment herself. 'I have perfect face structure and perfect teeth,' and even brag about a strong grip that ran in her family. Hundreds of times he would hear her say, regarding her family name, 'The _____s are strong people.'

She would use any misfortune and milk it to the ultimate. Her dad passed away after a long illness. Long after the death, she milked many for sympathy, extracting sympathy to the point of turning failing grades into passing grades from several professors.

She knew how to get people out of her way. She would boldly go to people who were running for an office she desired in the school that she attended, and would talk them out of running. She would use persuasive and skillful language, saying things such as 'This is too much work for you.'

When he sought counsel and decided to break up with her, she begged him not to. But the very second she realized his decision was made, he became her worst enemy.

The sweetness and devoted love instantly turned vicious, and she declared hatred for him beyond belief. She used filthy language, calling him hateful and vile names. Yet they were both Christians and, in his long explanation of the break up, he stated again and again that his decision was the result of much prayer.

For two years she worked to destroy him. She, manifesting borderline clairvoyancy, would seem to know whom he was attempting to date. She would quickly befriend the young lady and begin to lie and make distortions about him, to such an extent that it was nearly impossible for him to get a date. She worked tirelessly to destroy his reputation.

What was his crime? He didn't submit to her wishes. He dared to not let her have what she wanted.

This girl was the last child of parents who were in their mid-forties when she was conceived. She had confided that she was never disciplined, and her daddy always gave her absolutely anything she wanted. She was not accustomed to being denied anything.

Jezebels hate the cross. The cross means denying one's self. No Jezebel wants that. They want power! They want control at any cost, no matter who is destroyed! After all, when being self-centered, no one is as important as they.

Common characteristics:
- Must accomplish her will (at anyone's expense)
- Excessive bragging
- Preoccupation with self
- Possessive love (turns from sweet to sour if she doesn't get her way)
- Vindictiveness if she doesn't get her way

Can Jezebels Be Set Free?

While we must have compassion for those who are bound with the spirit of Jezebel, we must also have compassion for those who have experienced irreparable damage by the operation of that spirit. Therefore, we must be firm to not agree with their ways and controlling tactics, and even be willing to confront them.

Through God's grace, He can bring people **to repentance of the pattern of control** and deliver them from any spirit who has a hold on them. God has called us to victory, and in His victory is freedom to make choices under His direction and not be subject to any control of man, but rather to be led by the Holy Spirit.

Repentance is the key. Those who have opened themselves to a Jezebel spirit, must not only feel sorry, but genuinely seek repentance.

Because of the deep pattern of control, which has become an imbedded life style, those recognizing this must be willing to **confront** the controller boldly, and specifically point out his actions. The weapon we have is truth (spoken in love, Ephesians 4:15), and it is truth that sets people free (John 8:32).

If the person under the Jezebel spirit responds to the confrontation and seeks repentance, he or she can be delivered. However, the person will also need to renounce the behavioral patterns of control in their personality, which may well go all the way back to childhood.

Some might suggest that a Jezebel spirit can simply be cast out. If it were only a demon, this is true. However, Jezebels have a personality that has been shaped by demonic thoughts of control. Flesh cannot be cast out. Neither can personality traits that are deeply entrenched. Therefore the person must be willing to ruthlessly face truth, and be willing to let God crucify his flesh. Subjecting the flesh and its patterns to the Holy Spirit must be done daily, in order for the person to be permanently set free.

There is always hope. God can and will bring deliverance!

Chapter 5

Eyes Open

My first experience with the spirit of control began with a bookkeeper. My wife and I had accepted an invitation to pastor a group of people who had begun meeting in a home.

Upon arriving in the city, we were informed that a neighboring pastor who was overseeing the group until we arrived, had done us the 'favor' of appointing a lady to be in charge of the bookkeeping until we had officially moved to the city.

This woman had a classic spirit of control, which became evident in our first few days in the city. This put me in an extremely awkward situation. Being only faintly acquainted with my new congregation, I was unable to replace her immediately without stirring up a lot of trouble.

Although my experience with controlling people was extremely limited, I was immediately aware that I had a problem on my hands.

Already she had volunteered to seek out housing for my wife and daughter and me. This, of course was a very needed thing, but her motive was evident; she wanted to be involved in the center of every decision concerning us, craving power and recognition.

Her husband was a typical Ahab (Ahab was the husband of Jezebel, who was manipulated by her during his reign as King) with a passive nature who had become tired of combating her incredible drive to be involved in everyone's life. He had totally abdicated his authority to her and buried himself in his work. He chose to be blind to the fact that she usurped his authority, and it was obvious he had lost all hope of her changing.

As is typical of a Jezebel, she was exuberantly helpful, volunteering for everything, almost to the point of replacing any need for anyone else at any time. There was no question that she wanted to be at the center of everything and privy to information that was none of her business.

Those with a Jezebel spirit have a need for power and to be the center of attention, and will pay just about any price for it.

Surprise!

The most eye-opening experience came just a few days after we arrived in town. The local pastor who had been overseeing things until we arrived, agreed to give me some guidance in getting the church off the ground. We arranged a private meeting to discuss the beginning strategy for this new group of people that had been meeting in a home. I was eager for his advice and input, and was looking forward to a private meeting at our apartment the following evening. When he arrived, we exchanged pleasantries, and began to discuss possible strategies for the new church. Only minutes had passed, when there was a knock at the door. To my amazement, it was this bookkeeper who just happened to feel 'a leading' to drop by. As it always seems to happen with a Jezebel, I was totally caught off-guard. This woman had no business in this meeting, but invited herself to stay for two hours, quickly interjecting her thoughts and desires for the newly born church into every portion of the discussion.

Looking back, I should have simply insisted that she leave, as it was a private meeting. But as a young pastor, I was so taken by surprise and, not knowing how to fully exert authority, I let her stay. I was appalled at her gall and audacity to intrude on the meeting however, and was angry at myself for not standing up to her. But even then, I knew that asking her to leave would have caused an ugly confrontation.

Clairvoyant

Jezebels are usually extremely clairvoyant. She 'knew' of this important meeting (with the assistance of a familiar spirit) and wanted to be on the inside.

She controlled in many other ways. For example, as a bookkeeper in this new found church, one of her duties was to prepare my salary check. However, each time my salary came due, she would dangle the check out in front of me, feigning a look as if she was the source of the money and was paying it out of her own resources. As a young pastor, this too caught me off guard. In retrospect, I realize I should have rebuked her and quickly reminded her she wasn't the source of the money. In fact, I should have refused to let her do this gloating altogether and insisted she leave the check in a designated place.

Controlling personalities have to feel in control even if they are not. They are often first to volunteer for responsibilities, because it gives them a platform on which to exert authority. Their motive is to work themselves into a position of influence. Although the person might be qualified, it is too high a price to pay to have such a person exercising authority. His motive is not pure and he will use it illegitimately. After years in the ministry, I personally believe any handling of money should be performed by an outside source (such as an accountant or hired layperson) who is a contented member of another church and one who is not personally involved with yours. People who have access to church finances often have to deal with a sense of power, and this can create an extremely unhealthy situation. God expects us to use wisdom and give no opportunity for the devil. This is an area where pastors need to seek the Lord for the proper way for the finances to be handled before appointing someone in that position. If the wrong person ends up with control of the finances, it is nearly impossible to get that control away from him without a hassle and a likely division in the church.

Although her check-writing methods seemed like a small thing, they revealed only the tip of the iceberg of the range of her controlling and manipulating personality.

Confrontation

Through prayer, things eventually came to a head. I caught her in several inconsistencies in her activities. I didn't handle it with the greatest of wisdom and, of course, the paper hit the fan.

When I relieved her of her duties, I tried to show love and handle things as professionally as possible, but the trouble had already begun.

Jezebels don't release power easily. She immediately began to draw sympathy from her family and all those in the church, whom she had already craftily intertwined in her life. It was amazing how she had sown damaging seed in so many lives, but was able to skillfully portray herself as the innocent person who had been betrayed. Taking on the spirit of a martyr, she quickly enlisted many in her 'cause'.

Confrontation is really the only 'cure' in dealing with a Jezebel spirit. The problem is that many leaders fear confrontation, knowing it will create an ugly scene. Therefore they prolong the inevitable. The unconfronted person's roots will go down deeper and more lives will be tainted until the person is ultimately confronted. Not only in churches, but in other Christian organizations there is often a person with a Jezebel spirit in a position of influence. This puts a tourniquet around the potential flow of the Spirit and thereby the fruitfulness of the Christian group. These Jezebels have usually worked their way up into the organization and because no one has confronted them along the way, they are seemingly immovable. Some have served in a position of power for so many years that their name is (in a very negative sense) synonymous with the organization itself. As an invited speaker to such places, I can feel the spirit of control towards me as well as over the people. Discerning Christians who could have potentially been a blessing to the organization, have not joined up, knowing it is under the influence of a strong Jezebel personality (male or female), and not the Holy Spirit.

God is doing some housecleaning in these days. Judgment begins at the household of God (1 Peter 4:17). He is removing those with the spirit of Saul and replacing them with such leaders as David, who have a heart after God, Himself. They have no agenda, or a need for recognition, only to be an instrument of blessing for the increase of the Kingdom of God.

Again, although we love the person, we have to deal **ruthlessly** with the spirit of Jezebel.

Three Types of Love

The person who operates with a Jezebel spirit usually has very twisted thinking where love and authority are concerned. In fact, one of the most deceptive characteristics is the manner in which a Jezebel 'loves' the person whom he or she is using for the wrong motives.

This 'love' is not a divine love, or even a refined human love. Rather it is a totally selfish love, with its own agenda, seeking recognition or control.

When confronted, or that twisted love is rejected, it is anything but divine. The selfishness and self-seeking of that love will be revealed, as the person turns on you with a vengeance.

Manipulative love says I'll do something for you if you do something for me. There are self-seeking motives and strings attached to this kind of love. Sadly, many are unaware when they are being manipulated. The manipulation is nothing more than actions required to get you to agree and conform to their wishes. Basically, you are being used.

Possessive love is a suffocating expression of love that promises anything. But total devotion is expected in return. Jezebels are not only demanding, but dominating and consuming of your time and attention. If you do not allow such persons to possess you, or dare to give your attention to someone or something other than them, they will turn on you with a vengeance.

Divine love gives and expects nothing in return. No strings attached. Divine love leaves you totally free to make your own decisions. Jesus Christ is the perfect expression of divine love.

Naturally, God desires that Christians mature into His divine love, abandoning selfish gain, motives and ambitions.

> *'But if you have bitter envy and **self-seeking** in your hearts, do not boast and lie against the truth. This wisdom does not descend from above, but is earthly, sensual and demonic. For where envy and **self-seeking** exist, confusion and every evil thing are there. But the wisdom that is from above is first pure, then peaceable, gentle, willing to yield, full of mercy and good fruits, without partiality and without hypocrisy.'*
>
> (James 3:14–17)

Beware, once you cross or confront a Jezebel spirit. This person who 'loved' you more than life itself, will now turn on you. The same power that 'loved' you now turns into an equal power devoted to destroying you and your reputation. The Jezebel, although the motive was twisted, now feels scorned and betrayed, and is going to go to **any** means to hurt you. Any confidences you made will now be used as weapons against you. Like Elijah running from Jezebel, you feel like running for cover, as the intimidation of that spirit is so powerful.

> *'Then Jezebel sent a messenger to Elijah, saying, "So let the gods do to me, and more also, if I do not make your life as the life of one of them by tomorrow about this time."*
>
> *And when he saw that, he arose and ran for his life, and went to Beersheba, which belongs to Judah, and left his servant there.'* (1 Kings 19:2–3)

With either sex it holds true. If you come against the spirit of control in either a male or female, you can expect retaliation. Those who control don't like to be wrong and hate to have their power base threatened.

Ammunition

Ammunition is another issue. Jezebels are continually collecting ammunition. They acquire information that they can use against you, in case they ever begin to lose their grip on power. Beware – anything confided to a controlling person, can and **will** be used against you later – without mercy. The Jezebels have a problem of insecurity and cannot tolerate rejection. Just in case you should ever contradict their desires, the ammunition is collected for retaliation purposes. Remember, a Jezebel will never admit to wrong doing. If you threaten its power and influence, it will seek to destroy you.

Why Did I Give That Information?

It is difficult to understand the 'spiritual' power that a Jezebel possesses. With this particular individual, for example, my wife and I would 'catch' ourselves offering personal information to her whenever she was around. To our dismay later, we would often realize that we had confided in her about matters and 'surrendered' information that she had no business knowing. There is something about the deceiving 'power' of that spirit that makes you feel that you almost 'owe' it information.

Looking back, it is obvious that this is nothing more than that spirit wanting control. The more information, especially personal information it has, the more vulnerable it leaves you to the wiles of the Jezebel. Frankly, the person can use that information as ammunition against you should he or she ever need it.

They're Trying to Steal My Microphone

During our first year and a half of serving as pastors, my wife and I were invited to speak in Phoenix, Arizona. The day before we were scheduled to return home, I had a dream. In the dream, I was standing behind the pulpit at our church, and a number of people stood around me, all grasping for my microphone. It erupted into a scuffle until I stood alone holding the microphone, with loose and disconnected wires dangling from it. Then a friend of mine who is greatly used by God in the gift of prophecy stepped forward and spoke something to the effect that God was going to take charge of the situation. Next in the dream, as I was still standing before the microphone, about thirty disgruntled people stood up and walked out of the back of the church. Then almost instantly, sixty or seventy came in, more than doubling those who had left. The dream ended.

We flew home the following day. When we arrived at the Sunday morning service, it was obvious something was amiss. Although we were the pastors, we did not feel welcome. The next two days were like a whirlwind. Many things came to the surface revealing jealousy and various factions among the people. I was accused of everything from being a one-man show, to a false prophet, to possibly the anti-Christ. The venom directed at me made no sense.

Looking back, I realized from the inception of the church there were a large number of people who had come with their own agenda, basically seeking position and power. When I wasn't quick to appoint them to any position they desired, the jealousy and opposition escalated, finally coming to a head while we were away in Arizona on a ministry trip.

In the days following I sought counsel from my pastor in Kansas City, as well as from many other ministers I looked to for spiritual direction and guidance. They all gave me similar wisdom and godly counsel regarding the situation.

Confrontation Time

When I returned to the pulpit on Sunday, I didn't preach, but made an opening confession. 'I don't know how to pastor a church.'

When I spoke the words, sighs of relief filled the auditorium. Then I continued, 'But neither do you know how to pastor a church; only the Holy Spirit does.' If they weren't ready for the first statement, they surely weren't ready for the second.

I spent the next thirty minutes exposing all the hearsay and clearing the air of all the gossip that had come to my ears. I didn't want the devil to have any darkness with which to function. *'God is light and in Him is no darkness at all'* (1 John 1:5). Then I restated our vision and purpose and made a point of not apologizing for the fact that God had called me to pastor that church. That day, I lost thirty people, coinciding with the prophetic dream God had given me. But exactly like the dream, we gained seventy more people (doubling the loss) by the following Sunday.

From that point we began to grow as a church. God's wisdom had gathered all the poison together and then purged it all at once. All those striving for control were now removed. Although we were not without difficulties, there was an atmosphere of health in the church, and the presence of God was manifest in a fresh and greater dimension.

It is God's Church

In another portion of the same dream God was correcting

me. As I stood before the people (right before the struggle began for my microphone) my pockets appeared to be bulging with paraphernalia. Various items were hanging out everywhere. It looked ridiculous. Then in very distinct letters in front of me was the word, **preoccupied**. In this part of the dream, God was clearly rebuking me. While he was indicating how He was going to deal with the spirit of control, He was telling me to get my priorities straight as a pastor. During those following weeks, I not only repented of being preoccupied, but took action to set my life in order. Like many pastors, I was absorbed with far too many insignificant details, and as the Holy Spirit had specifically pointed out, I was distracted and preoccupied. He is the Head of the church and He corrects leadership, as well as the entire body of Christ.

Two Sides

There are always two sides of the coin. Many times leaders think they are exempt from correction. While God is setting things in order, He will correct leadership, as well as those who are rebellious against authority. It is of utmost importance to remain teachable, to have the heart of a servant, not a tyrant.

Ego probably stands in the way more than any other factor in leadership.

When ego has not been dealt with, a leader begins to think of himself as without fault or flaws. Jesus is our example and, frankly, He opposes the proud. *'God resists the proud, but gives grace to the humble'* (1 Peter 5:5).

I have seen some of the most blatant acts of control emanating from the pulpit. Control through manipulation and intimidation and fear has been used to trap people in a church, or in an abusive situation, which is an illegitimate use of divine authority.

A leader must be a broken vessel; one whose will has been surrendered to God, so he stands in God's authority, not his own. Unbroken vessels tend to dominate people in order to keep them under their control for the sake of their own agenda.

When God breaks the will, one can legitimately stand in His authority, because he is **under** His authority.

There is no greater freedom than being under God's authority. We are free from having to defend ourselves and to seek our own agenda. We know that we have no rights because He has purchased our lives with His own blood. We stand free to serve. God is an awesome Master, and He knows how to take care of His own.

Chapter 6

Controllers and Insecurity

'If you have found something you love, release it and let it go. If it comes back to you, it was meant for you.' – If it does not, **hunt it down and kill it**.

Two things have always plagued the church – control and the desire to dominate. This power struggle has always been what divides and short-circuits the power of the church.

The desire to control and dominate, if not mastered, can lead to witchcraft, since witchcraft is nothing more than illegitimately controlling the will of another person.

Witchcraft, which is a work of the flesh (Galatians 5:20), manifests basically in three ways – **manipulation**, **intimidation**, and **domination**.

Witchcraft is illegitimate authority!

The reason the desire to control is akin to witchcraft is that it is in total contradiction to the nature of God Himself. The irrevocable gift God gave to mankind is that of a free will. God, Himself, refuses to violate His gift of our free will. He will woo us, draw us, and attempt to lead us, but He always leaves it up to us to **choose** His way.

> *'I call heaven and earth as witnesses today against you, that I have set before you life and death, blessing and cursing; therefore* **choose life**, *that both you and your descendants may live.'* (Deuteronomy 30:19)

God will love people to their grave, desiring to woo them to Himself, but He will never force His purpose on any man. He will in no way force eternal life or heaven on any person. He honors our 'right' to choose.

Therefore, when people try to manipulate or dominate the will of others, it is in direct violation of God's laws and comes under Satan's domain, namely witchcraft.

Manipulation

The most cunning and yet common way the spirit of control operates is through manipulation. This usually comes across as 'If you do this for me, I'll do this for you.' Manipulation **always** has a motive with it. It is used in countless ways, such as flattery, self-pity, hinting for something, etc. It begins in simple ways. For example, a child who throws a tantrum to get his own way. He may manipulate his parents in front of other adults by throwing a fit at an opportune time, cleverly manipulating them, knowing they won't (although they should) take action with company present.

In marriages it takes on another form, usually manifesting through means of the silent treatment, dignified pouting or sulking. There may be a withholding of sex by the wife, or using seductive charms to get what she wants. The husband may withhold finances, or find countless other manipulative acts to get his way. There is nothing more repulsive than a man who puts his wife down, especially in front of other people. Men who do this have such poor self-esteem, that they have to belittle their wives to make themselves feel better.

A major power wielder (through a spouse) is the threat of suicide. Many wives have stayed in a destructive marriage because the selfish, manipulative, and egocentric husband cries, 'If you leave me, I'll kill myself.' Not wanting to be responsible for a death, the naive spouse, yielding to a sickening fear, accepts this form of manipulation and decides to stay, in spite of emotional and physical abuse and unprecedented misery.

In the ministry, manipulation is an often wielded tool to put guilt on people. 'Send money to this ministry, or I am going off the air, and the blood will be on your hands.' Or, 'You must give if you expect God to bless you.' The use of manipulation to extract money comes in many forms, but all manipulation is evil in that it illegitimately controls people into the response the person desires. Additionally it side-steps and hinders the Person of the Holy Spirit to speak to people to give as He moves on them. The principles and blessings of giving fill the entire Bible, but people must have the freedom to be moved on by the Holy Spirit where and when to give, and not be manipulated into a response.

Intimidation

The second method of control is through intimidation and fear. This usually carries with it the threat of losing something such as, 'If you want to keep your job,' or 'If you want to remain in this marriage,' you must do such and such. Any time this person is not sure of his position or his authority, he always relies on intimidation. A boss may intimidate employees simply through a raised eyebrow that implies if you don't go along with my action, there will be consequences.

Intimidation always seeks to move the person through threats. This use of fear, puts the victim under control out of fear of losing something precious to him (like his life).

Fear is used by intimidators to paralyze the person to capture a specific response. This intimidation and fear are blatantly the use of control, through exercising illegitimate authority.

Domination

The third and most drastic method of control is simply

through dominating the will of another person. This is the most dastardly type of control, because it leaves the person being controlled no option. Husbands use this method over battered wives, not letting them out of their sight, or threatening injury or death if they attempt to leave.

A person with a dominating personality makes you feel suffocated and literally powerless to disagree. Victims feel so controlled by the threat of disapproval or violence or a scathing rebuke, that they fear to speak up. These controllers usually contradict everything you say. You know no matter what statement you make, it will be disputed. If you say, 'It is two o'clock,' the controller will say, 'No, it is three minutes past two.' A controller will also continually point out tiny flaws. Their low self-esteem seems to gain a notch by finding imperfections in you.

Why Do People Become Controllers?

Controllers usually come from the ranks of those who have been controlled. They've learned it through someone doing it to them.

Many women who have been abused by men, whether a father, a grandfather, or an uncle, are often trying to get back at men because they feel they have been victims. Living in a male-dominated world, often without the love and protection legitimately needed, they seek to protect themselves by becoming just like it. Rather than feel like they are being controlled, they learn to control – their desire being to live in some fashion unabused and protected from the harshness of men, who have not been gentle and loving.

Since a woman is not as strong as a man, she becomes skilled at charms and seductions, temper throwing, and putting a man down. Without using physical force she can learn to position herself in a way to be in control. But in reality she is submitting to the Jezebel spirit and her thoughts are being structured by it. This person may not necessarily have a Jezebel spirit, but may have a thought structure that helps a Jezebel spirit easily find a home. A certain number of women have had some measure of this put on them as they are growing up.

This spirit, in full maturity, is in total rebellion against God and tries to turn everything into the opposite of what God intended. The spirit so resents men that it ultimately identifies God as the source of putting men 'over' women. Basically it hates all order that God has set up in life. In its full expression, it tries to make men into women. Jezebel surrounded herself with eunuchs. It tries to make men into homosexuals. It seeks to turn men into women – the hair, the clothes, the lack of masculinity, the effeminate voice, and so forth.

In the church, it comes subtly. It comes in with a false ministry. If the person has a prophetic gift, he or she uses it illegitimately to gain a following of people around him or her that he or she can control. Flattery is a common method to gain control, playing on the insecurity of others. This is nothing more than manipulation in order to build a platform to gain control into the church.

True prophetic giftings operate from humility and accountability, and not control and manipulation. The desire and purpose of manipulation is to draw people in.

Although there is flattery in public, there is criticism in private. That spirit seeks to tear down, in order to elevate itself. The person has a determination to be recognized and seeks to have authority.

True Ministry

Those who control love recognition. True ministry never labels itself, but lets people discover it on their own. If you have a genuine call of God, let people recognize it. Don't wear a badge.

If you have a prophetic gift, let people recognize it. Don't cheapen yourself by sticking the label on yourself.

Why take it so personally if prophetic words or wisdom

from God weren't recognized or received? These types of people will usually leave or threaten to leave a church because their 'ministry' isn't received. But consider a mail carrier. You never see a postman sitting on the curb, crying, because you received a bill in the mail. No – he is only the deliverer of the message. The Lord revealed to me that if you are upset over how people received your 'message', that is an indication the message came from you and not from God. If it is God's message, He should be the one upset, not you. You are not in charge, God is.

The Need for Predictability

Control also rises from the desire to see things **predictable** at every stage of life. Seeking predictability leads to control, in that a person becomes manipulative of circumstances, so that he or she always has everything in its place. Somewhere fear has entered this person and the result is extreme insecurity. The less predictable a situation is, the more insecure the person feels. Great effort is spent on manipulating people and circumstances so nothing is left to chance. This person is not only lacking trust in God, but is in a position of being hostile toward God, who is seen as a guilty party in not cooperating with the predictable desires.

How Control Takes Root

The most common cause of the controlling personality is fear and insecurity. Insecurity is the root of the spirit of control. It is the deepest root cause of all problems of fear, jealousy, anger, resentment and control.

Those plagued with insecurity have a great sense of rejection and are seeking attention and approval. The complexity of insecurity and inferiority comes to a head in the desire to control. Finding the feelings of inferiority intolerable (often in one who feels his physical body doesn't measure up) the mentality flip flops into a sense of superiority and pride. This twisted pride runs even deeper than the typical ego of an athletic jock. This person who once felt so deeply inferior, now in a perverted sense feels superior to everyone. He is now a know-it-all and is threatened by everyone (who would dare to disagree) seeing them as the enemy. He now has the answer to everything and is characteristically extremely opinionated. He's quick to express his opinion as the final authority. No input needed. Thank you.

The power of control gives the insecure a feeling of self-worth and importance. It gives validity to their existence. The pattern begins at a young age and develops into a life-style. That is why it is so rare to see those with a controlling spirit totally delivered. Controlling has become such a part of their nature; it literally becomes their personality.

There is a consistent correlation between those with a low self-esteem and a determination to control others. With the feeling of poor self-worth comes such a spirit of rejection that the only way the person perceives obtaining acceptance, recognition or power is through the vehicle of control. You can almost hear the controller reason, 'I'm sick of low self-worth and rejection, so I will be in control of every person in my path, and no one will ever make me feel this way again.'

Pride

The stronghold of pride is closely tied with insecurity. Since the controller can't stand the rejection of being wrong, he will more and more build up a stronghold of pride. Words like, 'I'm sorry,' or 'It was totally my fault,' will never pass his lips. So many times I have counseled a husband or wife who is married to a controller. It is always the same. The controller, in years of marriage, has never admitted he or she was wrong about anything. Usually the one without the spirit of control will express how many times he or she has admitted being wrong, just to bring peace, but then resents how the controller, under no circumstances, will admit wrongdoing of any kind. Saying reluctant words to the effect, 'I'm sorry you misunderstood me,' is the admission of nothing, and further reinforces pride and an unteachable spirit.

Boastful

Closely tied to pride is the characteristic of boasting. Again rooted in insecurity and rejection, the controller has to remind everyone how successful his life is, what great accomplishments his children have made, and on and on. Of course as he boasts, he is not even remotely interested in the achievements of those listening. He is desperately trying to elevate himself in his own mind.

Fear of Rejection

Controllers are bound with a fear of rejection. Characteristically, their life has to be perfect. Therefore, you may observe a strong preoccupation with looks, clothes, makeup, jewelry, cars, cleanliness. Bound with a fear of rejection, this controller cannot consider the thought of being seen in public as less than perfect. Therefore, his or her environment is carefully chosen in order to never be perceived by anyone as less than perfect. This of course, is far from freedom.

Aren't All Insecure?

Not everyone who is insecure is a controlling person. The truth is, that we all have a measure of insecurity within us. No doubt it goes all the way back to Adam and Eve when, upon sinning, they initially experienced insecurity and tried to hide from God (Genesis 3).

We live in an insecure world. We strive to dress, to own possessions, to attain power, to find acceptance, all to fulfill an insecure void within us.

Criticism is rooted in insecurity. **Criticizing others**

elevates the insecure person in his own mind. Hearing praise of the accomplishments of another person usually causes a reaction in the insecure. It makes the insecure feel less of a person and fragile in his own esteem. Quickly, he will say something to upgrade his own accomplishments, in view of what has been spoken in praise of another person.

Insecurity needs to be taken to the cross. The security of every believer is to be in the person of Jesus Christ.

When we are secure in Christ, and let Him deliver us from our insecurities, we are freed. We relinquish all rights to our lives and lay them at the foot of the cross. We walk away free!

In Christ, we declare our helplessness and receive His acceptance. *'To the praise of the glory of His grace, by which He made us **accepted** in the Beloved'* (Ephesians 1:6).

His unconditional love annihilates all rejection and we are free in Him. No longer do we perceive His love for us tied to our performance, but His love saturates our being, knowing we are loved and accepted in spite of any flaws or failures.

If we fear (and need to control) we haven't yet received His love.

> *'There is no fear in love; but perfect love casts out fear, because fear involves torment. But he who fears **has not been made perfect in love**.'*　　　　(1 John 4:18)

What Motivates Controllers?

- They cannot stand to be wrong.
- They have a need to be elevated, awarding themselves credit and even titles.
- They have a need to feel power and authority, and will do anything to achieve it.
- They feel they know more than anyone, therefore they dominate all conversations.
- They feel no one can handle things as well as they (even God). Therefore they take things into their own hands.

The Youngest Child

Sometimes the youngest child of a family falls victim to developing a spirit of control, simply because he was spoiled. The parents, seeing that it is the last baby to be raised in the home have a tendency to over-protect, and over-indulge the child, even to the point of rarely exerting discipline. Common behaviors are letting the child get his way, cooking separate meals for the child because he doesn't like the food the rest of the family is eating, not enforcing bedtimes, withholding discipline, lavishing on the child anything he asks for, and basically letting him manipulate.

Tragically, the child grows up to be a classic manipulator. Although there is a low self-esteem (because undisciplined children often have low self-esteem, as discipline done in love builds self-esteem and self-worth), the child-now-adult projects a false sense of importance and an 'I can do no wrong attitude.'

Those who have been severely spoiled will let nothing stand in their way to accomplish their desires.

Often, while the other grown siblings watch, the child who was spoiled (now grown) will take advantage of aging parents. For example, we recently counseled in a situation where the youngest girl insisted her parents baby-sit her children for long periods of time, although the parents were elderly and in very poor health. When the older siblings tried to object, they were scorned and tongue-lashed. In another situation, the youngest sibling manipulated the elderly parents by continually asking for money for various ventures, although the parents were on a very limited income. These people generally get what they want and have honed their skills in manipulating and getting people to do what they want. They don't care who they hurt in the process, being totally self-serving. Growing up, they learned to get their own way through manipulation, pouting, tantrum throwing, sulking, threats, and intimidation. Achieving the ability to get their own way, they became professional controllers. Now they use more refined tactics, as the behavior and the evil spirit are deeply and firmly planted.

Why Deliverance Doesn't Come

When the insecure is confronted with truth, he perceives the confronter as the enemy. Then he 'counter attacks' with assaults against this 'enemy'.

In fact, no greater wrath seems to occur than when a controlling person is confronted. This person will never admit guilt or relinquish the sense of power, and will retaliate against the confronter.

Defensiveness is a common reaction when a suggestion is made. This again is out of insecurity. Insecurity, deep rooted, cannot take correction, because **all correction is perceived as rejection**. Therefore, you will never find a person with a controlling spirit ever admitting he is wrong. It is always the fault of someone else. Never is there a confession of guilt, contrition, or true remorse. The closest controllers come to apologizing is, 'I'm sorry you misunderstood me.'

If you insist on an apology and confront the controller, you will probably get a screaming response such as, 'Yes, I'm wrong, I'm always wrong. I'm a total failure.' This sarcastic spewing is a long way from repentance. The loud volume and sarcasm in the voice is the person telling you, 'I'm still in control.'

Is a Jezebel Spirit Only in Women?

It is ridiculous and shallow to think that the spirit of Jezebel only operates through the female sex. In fact, it seems to manifest even more through the male.

Leaders who are insecure are notorious for using a heavy hand to control. The insecure and fearful blatantly lack trust in God to be their source, so they begin to rule over people, giving those around them no freedom to disagree.

One major characteristic of a controller is that he has to be right. He has no tolerance for being wrong, and will rarely, if ever, admit to wrong doing. In a dialogue, he will twist things around to the point of making you feel you need to apologize for causing him to make a bad decision.

Another characteristic is that the controller will always take credit for anything that looks good. He will quickly overlook those who did the hard work and step on people, sacrificing all etiquette to be the one who receives credit.

These controllers rarely give praise and affirmation, because, in their eyes, it is lowering themselves from their position of exaltation. I wonder how these leaders twist the biblical admonition, *'Yet it shall not be so among you; but whoever desires to become great among you, let him be your servant'* (Matthew 20:26).

Switching Curses?

With the desire to reject the 'bondage' that society has put on them, women can take on man's curse. Feminists, wanting to be like men, end up putting themselves under the 'sweat of the brow' and living under pressure never meant for them. They end up living under stress and strain and even a responsibility that God doesn't require of them.

This in turn happens to men. Rejecting the 'curse' of their responsibilities, they surrender their masculinity, desiring to live in a woman-oriented world, taking on feminine traits, living without the fulfillment God intended for them.

Jesus Was in an Abusive Situation

Jesus was in an abusive situation preceding Calvary, but He committed Himself to His Father. He chose to entrust His life to the Father's hands, not taking things into His own hands.

'Who, when He was reviled, did not revile in return; when He suffered, He did not threaten, but committed Himself to Him who judges righteously.' (1 Peter 2:23)

Controllers don't want to leave things to God. They want to bring it to pass on their own. Not trusting God to vindicate them, they seek to control, justifying their actions as 'doing it to others, before they do it to you.'

The Holy Spirit is an enabler. He helps us to overcome all obstacles. He teaches us to put our trust in God.

'Behold, I lay in Zion, a chief cornerstone, elect, precious, and he who believes on Him will by no means be put to shame.' (1 Peter 2:6)

Chapter 7

Characteristics of a Jezebel Spirit

Below are listed a number of significant traits of the Jezebel spirit that my wife and I have observed in a variety of situations. The traits are amazingly consistent, although the circumstances may not be even remotely related. The 'character' of the devil doesn't change and therefore the characteristics of control remain consistent.

Naturally it is not fair to pick one or two traits and determine that one is dealing with a Jezebel spirit. All people have character flaws and blind spots. However, when a number of these traits coincide, it is easy to conclude that one is dealing with the spirit and personality of a Jezebel.

Is Jezebel a spirit or a work of the flesh? Jezebel is a spirit, but it has found access through uncrucified flesh.

1. Refuses to admit guilt or wrong

A Jezebel spirit is never wrong, unless it is a temporary admittance of guilt to gain 'favor' with someone. To accept responsibility would violate the core of insecurity and pride they operate from. When a Jezebel apologizes, it is **never** in true repentance or acknowledgement of wrong doing, but rather 'I'm sorry your feelings were hurt.'

2. Uses people to accomplish their agenda

It lets others do their dirty work. The Jezebel gets another person's emotions stirred up, then lets that person go into a rage. The Jezebel sits back looking innocent, saying, 'Who me? What did I do?' This behavior makes it difficult for even the most ardent truth seekers to pin one down. The Jezebel is clever in its agenda.

3. Withholds information

This is a form of control. He wields power over you by knowing something you don't know in a situation. In the eyes of a Jezebel, having information you don't have is a powerful weapon of control.

4. Talks in confusion

It is impossible to converse with the person in logic. One pastor wrote a six page letter to his elders about a situation in the church. The context was so vague, no one was without confusion. This is a way to maintain control and domination. When confronting a Jezebel, the subject may be changed five times in one minute. Confusion keeps them 'undiscovered' and unexposed.

5. Volunteers for anything

Jezebels volunteer in order to establish control. They seemingly have endless (nervous) energy and eagerly look for opportunities to be in charge of projects. Although they will work hard, their motive is never pure, and eventually their secret agenda cannot be hidden.

6. Lies

Convincingly. No one can lie better than Jezebels. They can turn on the charm and make you believe blue is red. They always fool those whom they've just met, while those who have been victimized by their tactics, stand by helplessly. To look you in the eye and lie, just shows how strong and adamant this rebellious and recalcitrant spirit is.

7. Ignores people

A classic ploy of a controller is when you disagree with him, he will ignore you. This is frequently used by leaders when someone doesn't agree with their plan, and they isolate the person by ignoring him, choosing not even to talk to him. Some in these situations have been ignored for months, just because they chose not to be a puppet and say yes to every idea or whim. This puts the person out of their grace and forces him to either 'come around' to their way of thinking or be indefinitely ignored. One is not free to disagree with a controller.

8. Never gives credit or shows gratitude

A Jezebel will rarely acknowledge another person's actions, even to something that turned out to greatly benefit the Jezebel. They just cannot bring themselves to say thank you, or to acknowledge that someone else did something right. There are those who have gone out of their way to bless a pastor or boss, by being the catalyst of sending him on a trip or giving a gift. Yet never will there be a thank you. This again puts the controller in a position of power.

9. Criticizes everyone

This is so characteristic of controllers. They have to be the one who looks good, so they will quickly sharply criticize anyone who makes a suggestion or plan. Even though they like the plan, they can only criticize it because the idea did not originate with them. Criticizing others, elevates the controller in his own mind.

10. One-upmanship

A person with a Jezebel spirit will always upstage another person. He feels threatened by anyone who dares to steal the limelight, or any person who is a threat to his power and control base. If you are with such a person and tell of your accomplishment or victory, you can be assured the Jezebel will quickly tell something he has accomplished.

11. Sequesters information

They love to be in control of information. If there is ever a situation where information is important, they will push to be the 'first' to know it. They seem to know everything about everyone. Where they get all their information is beyond comprehension, but they can dictate to you data and details about lives and actions of people in mass quantities.

12. Uses information

They use information as a leverage for power and then share tidbits with you, often things told them in confidence. This gives them a sense of power, even to the point of impressing people that they know things about people that others do not.

13. Talks incessantly

Many people talk habitually, but a Jezebel uses talking as a form of control. In a typical conversation, he does all the talking, whether it is about sports, the weather, or the Kingdom of God. Because of this form of control, he is unable to receive input from anyone in his life. All conversation with him is one sided. You are doing the **listening**.

14. Spiritualizes everything

This is a common thing a controller does when he or she is confronted. They spiritualize the situation, explaining it off on God. This prevents them from owning up to responsibility required of them. The implication is always, 'You've got a problem, I don't.'

15. Insubordination

They never take the side of the employer or a person in authority, unless it is a temporary action to make themselves look good. They often will take credit for someone else's idea. Their main desire is for power and control. There is no conscience when an opportunity for recognition presents itself.

16. Is pushy and domineering

Always pressures you to do things, seemingly ripping from you your right to choose, or make a decision for yourself. They make others feel as though they don't have enough sense to think for themselves.

17. Is clairvoyant

Many of those who operate with a spirit of control also have a clairvoyant spirit. They have supernatural help in knowing and sensing information through a clairvoyance they have acquired. If they use this against you, they may say, 'I can't tell you how I know this, I just know it.' This is not the Holy Spirit, but the help of a clairvoyant or familiar spirit. Clairvoyance may be defined as the power to perceive things that are out of the range of human senses.

18. Uses the element of surprise

Their main thrust is to be in control and a large part of control is catching you off guard. Therefore, the element of surprise works well when they show up a day early for a meeting, etc.

19. Sows seeds of discord

A Jezebel will continually belittle another person, in the most subtle way. The strategy is to 'gain' control by minimizing the worth and value of another person. It is common for him to tell half-truths to implicate another person in your eyes. Sowing these seeds, he hopes to eventually reap a harvest of destruction, improving his position of power.

20. Commands attention

They like to be the center of attention and don't like to see others recognized and lauded. When that happens they will quickly undermine the person's accomplishments verbally.

21. *Is vengeful*

Since Jezebels are never wrong, if you contradict or confront one, get ready to become his worst enemy. As long as you are in agreement with him, all is fine. But if you confront or challenge one, then look out. You are the target of its fiercest venom. A Jezebel will stop at nothing to destroy your reputation.

22. *Attempts to make you look like you're the Jezebel*

A Jezebel spirit is difficult to pin down. If the person is near to being confronted, he or she will skillfully twist the entire situation, trying to make the innocent person look like the one who is attempting to control. As always, the Jezebel will do anything to look like the one who is right.

23. *Insinuates disapproval*

A Jezebel will often imply disapproval to those under its control. The person controlled feels no freedom to express an opinion, for fear of disapproval. This often manifests in a marriage or in a working environment.

24. *Knows it all*

A Jezebel is usually blatant regarding his knowledge of everything. Quick to express his opinion in any area, he leaves little room for anyone to point out the other side of an issue. Has idols of his opinions.

25. *Is ambitious*

Strong desire, but all for self. 'I want what I want, when I want it,' describes his worship of self-will. A Jezebel leader will never use the words, 'We have a vision,' but rather, 'My vision is thus and so.'

26. *Gift giving*

This form of manipulation always makes you feel obligated to them. It also compromises the victim in speaking direct and confrontive truth. Naturally, not everyone who gives gifts is guilty of control, but it is a tactic used by those who have a need to control.

27. *Is independent*

No one has input in his or her life. Fraternizes with no one unless it is to get you to 'cooperate' with his agenda.

28. *Is religious*

Dwells in the local church but doesn't like authority unless it is in the position of authority.

29. *Hides*

We all want to believe that the person with a Jezebel spirit is delivered. The person may seem 'normal' for a period, exhibiting none of the classic traits. Then suddenly without warning a situation will arise, once again with the spirit taking control and wreaking havoc over lives. Hopefully, true repentance will come. Only then will the person be delivered.

The good news is that God gives each individual person the freedom of choice. Everyone has the freedom to make decisions, to make mistakes, to think for himself, to communicate, to like or dislike and to express his taste and creativity.

Those who control are in worship of their will and their way. Thank God for freedom.

What Can We Do?

Can a person with a Jezebel spirit come to repentance? Yes. But the person must recognize the pattern and motive of control. Those with a Jezebel spirit must be confronted by someone who is not afraid of a reaction. If the person with that spirit is confronted about his actions in firmness and love, he may be able to recognize the spirit and seek deliverance. Without confrontation, the person no doubt will remain in the pattern of control, as it has become a lifestyle and there is no motivation to change.

Even following confrontation, the person may repent and acknowledge that he or she has a problem. But as often is the case, it is like the air-filled dolls that have sand in the bottom. When you punch them, they bounce right back upright. This spirit, and pattern of control doesn't let go easily. It must be dealt with ruthlessly.

Beyond deliverance from a demon, there must be a willingness to allow the Holy Spirit to bring change in one's personality. Patterns of control are often deeply entrenched in the personality by demonic thoughts shaping and forming a stronghold over time. Therefore, there must be not only the resistance of the devil, but a continual renouncing of all thought patterns that lead to control.

If you recognize any of these traits in your own life, begin by praying this prayer.

Prayer

> Father, I acknowledge that I have yielded myself to the spirit of Jezebel. I come to you, humbling myself before you. I desire your standard of righteousness and holiness. I ask you to forgive me for my tolerance of the Jezebel spirit and for being sympathetic to its ways.
>
> Please forgive me for every way I have opened myself to this spirit. Help me to ruthlessly reject every type of this thinking and the desire to control and manipulate other people. I renounce and bind this demon of Jezebel and I pull down this stronghold in my life. Through the Holy Spirit I will live by your standard of righteousness, holiness and conduct. Open my eyes and cause Your light to expose any darkness, and help me to walk in humility and truth. In Jesus' Name. Amen.

Chapter 8

The Spirit of Jezebel
Through Those in Authority

The most common weakness in those serving as leaders is that of insecurity. Those who are insecure are easily threatened by anyone who could potentially question their position or authority. This insecurity or fear is over-compensated by actions to keep people under their grip of control.

A leader who has a propensity toward control must guard against the temptation to isolate himself, and become authoritarian and relentless and obstinate in dominating the church. These types will often refuse accountability and become critical of all other leadership, isolating themselves from fellowship.

Often a controlling pastor had a dad or relative who was abused by a church board, and therefore he is bracing himself against similar abuse.

Using Fear and Bondage

Because some leaders are unable to 'keep' people solely with the presence of God, they resort to fear and bondage. For example, statements are often used to illegitimately wield authority. 'If you leave this church, you will be without a spiritual covering.' This is often effective because it wraps people in a spirit of fear. But fear should **never** motivate a believer, only love. The reason the principle of submission, as it is preached through legalistic thinking, produces death, is because it has no foundation of love. It is likened to erecting a wall of a building without first pouring a concrete foundation. The wall will eventually crumble. '... *For the letter kills, but the Spirit gives life'* (2 Corinthians 3:6).

Any time people preach submission to authority, loyalty and commitment without basing it on the foundation of love, it will produce robot-like believers bound by fear, not saints grounded in love.

> 'That Christ may dwell in your hearts through faith; that you, being **rooted and grounded in love** ...'
>
> (Ephesians 3:17)

The Tactics of Man ... How Can God Be Pleased?

A common way that those who are building their own kingdom bring increase to their ranks, is simple. They don't wait on God to add to the church. They give newcomers an instant title instead. Visitors to their churches are approached almost immediately and given a job. The naive and innocent quickly succumb to the temptation. 'Finally, a place that needs me,' they reason. But they are only victims of a tactic to increase members. Once given a job title (menial as it may be) they feel obligated to stay and 'serve'. So the church has accomplished its task. They just added a new member. Although it was done illegitimately, they don't care. To them, it is just like building a business and accumulating clients. Perhaps it is, in God's eyes, a business too, and what they are doing has nothing to do with building His church. It is only building a religious organization with a religious name. As God said to the church at Sardis, *'You have a name that you are alive, but you are dead'* (Revelation 3:1).

Cream Rises to the Top

On one occasion I was wisely counseled by an experienced and seasoned pastor who said, 'You can't appoint people to positions, only God can. Your part is to watch the cream rise to the top. As you see God put His approval and anointing on someone, then you simply agree with God.'

No man can call another man to any type of ministry. Only God can. Naturally, a pastor might appoint deacons, ushers, and church workers, but no man can appoint an elder, only God can. The pastor can only recognize the calling God has already put on the man. A true elder should be an extension of the pastoral leadership, capable of hearing God, and able to preach and teach. His character should be one of stability, loyalty and faithfulness (1 Timothy 3:1–7). Neither can any man appoint anyone called to the five-fold ministry of the apostle, prophet, evangelist, pastor or teacher (Ephesians 4:11).

Yet sadly many of the elders in churches are men who are selected by men, not chosen and appointed by God. Because man judges outwardly, many are chosen by the carnal mind of the pastor who recognizes their business skills, success in their profession, popularity, prestige, friendliness, and so forth, but neglects to see the most vital ingredient which is their spiritual maturity and development. Although of adult physical stature, spiritually they are toddlers.

How Does God Count Growth?

Man counts growth by looking at things outwardly. He counts numbers of warm bodies, filling large buildings. God does not! God counts the growth in the maturing of individual Christians. When individual Christians are developing in their own spirit, learning to hear from God, endeavoring to yield up their carnal thoughts to receive God's thoughts, and discerning the ways of God, then the church is growing. God doesn't build churches. He builds people. People are the church. The number of people who pack buildings, often who are manipulated and coerced by man to become a part of their growing organization called a 'church', does not necessarily have anything to do with the increase of the Kingdom of God. Sometimes the 'successful' church has sacrificed its potential intimacy with God for more of a crowd-pleasing format.

I've heard well-known ministers state publicly that if a church is not having enormous mega growth, it doesn't have the blessing of God. To the contrary, the opposite may be true. First of all, not every church is destined to be large any more than every family is destined to be large. While men in their carnality only measure by numbers, many smaller churches have raised up quality ministries and sent them forth. Additionally, many small churches support a large proportion of outreaches, letting God use them as a funnel to distribute His provision to these needy places. Again, many who are large in numbers may consist of those who refuse to mature spiritually. A nursery may be full, but the 'members' are a long way from college graduation. God measures how His Kingdom is being increased in individuals, not how many believers are crammed into one building.

Some groups of people have decided to pay a higher price for the vision God has given them. Multitudes don't exactly flock to places where the Holy Spirit has required that people pay the high price of giving up their self-will. Jesus spent a lot of time investing Himself in only twelve disciples.

We all love to see expansion, and numerical growth is wonderful as long as God is bringing the increase.

If You Don't Agree with Me, You're Rebellious

One way those with the spirit of control operate is to quickly label anyone who doesn't submit to their authority as rebellious. This at times is true. There are some who can submit nowhere and have been a part of many churches. However, there are times to give credit to the people of God who are not stupid. For example, when the spirit is quenched time after time, when people are manipulated to give an offering, when the pulpit is used for the pastor to ventilate his 'side' of an issue without giving the people an opportunity to think for themselves, people may be wise not to submit to such leadership.

Let me make a pertinent point. The purpose of the pulpit is to feed the sheep (God's people). Problems with disgruntled people should be handled in a called meeting. People feel violated when a scathing sermon is given with attacks directed against obvious members. Frequently the sermon subject will revolve around the rebellion of Korah (Numbers 16). If the pastor is secure in God, he can confront any rebellion in a called meeting and give the people a chance to ventilate their concerns and disappointments.

Standing in the pulpit and spewing his frustrations, is not only the wrong place, but cowardly, and improper order and etiquette.

Pastors with Ego

There is nothing that gets in God's way more than ego. A wonderful acronym for ego is, Easing. God. Out.

There are some pastors who are excellent teachers and preachers of the Word of God, but much of their gift is eclipsed by their ego. Rather than seeing themselves as a servant whom God has called to lay down his life for the sheep, they see themselves as a Chief Executive Officer of a large company. God sees them more as the butler. God is the Chief Executive Officer.

Frankly, they boss people around, running the church like a business, rather than the Kingdom of God. To say the least, there is a great need for humility.

I believe God gives a man in the office of a pastor a legitimate authority. He shouldn't have to apologize for the position God has called him to. He shouldn't have to ask the church board for permission to invite a certain guest ministry, or have to seek permission from a committee to buy a minor purchase for the church.

However, neither should he abuse his power and position. There are pastors who never had much success financially before they were called into the ministry. But now, although they could never manage their own money, they have no problem spending the church's money to an extreme.

For example, I've met pastors who spend hours on the phone with long distance calls, talking leisurely to friends in the ministry just for fellowship. I can't help questioning if they were paying the phone bill, and not the church, would they spend an hour on a daytime long-distance call to a friend?

Some never had a decent automobile before their pastoral appointment, but they are not reluctant to trade cars every year, freely squandering the church's money. A group of people approached me recently regarding their pastor who had purchased five new cars in the last three years, totally at the expense of the church.

Pastors with ego protect their ego. They become unapproachable and label anyone as the enemy who would dare to question an abuse of finances.

Two Sides

This is not to agree with those who have a poverty spirit, who love to control leadership by refusing to bless them financially. If we are generous and bless our leaders, God will bless us accordingly. There are those who balk at every leader who dares to move ahead with a vision. The vision God gives will require risk-taking and finances.

There are two sides to this issue of authority. In countless churches, congregations have kept their pastors as paupers, never treating them with respect nor as laborers worthy of their hire. The deacons and elders are under a spirit of control, using manipulation to 'keep the pastor humble.' But we are to honor those who labor among us.

> *'Let the elders who rule well be counted worthy of double honor, especially those who labor in the word and doctrine. For the Scripture says, "You shall not muzzle an ox while it treads out the grain," and "The laborer is worthy of his wages."'* (1 Timothy 5:17–18)

> *'Remember those who rule over you, who have spoken the word of God to you, whose faith follow, considering the outcome of their conduct.'* (Hebrews 13:7)

> *'Obey those who rule over you, and be submissive, for they watch out for your souls, as those who must give account. Let them do so with joy and not with grief, for that would be unprofitable for you.'* (Hebrews 13:17)

There are leaders who abuse. Thank God He looks at the heart. He hates ego, pride and arrogance. God is generous. He will lavish blessings on people, even those we consider the most undeserving; but He does resist the proud (1 Peter 5:5). There is no place for ego in the Kingdom of God.

Some leaders mistake ego for authority. They don't understand that respect must be earned. Jesus is our example. He laid down His life for the sheep. Authority is best described as service, not bossing people around, but rather as a father of a family who guides his children into adulthood. A true father is a servant.

There is nothing more detestable in a leader than ego and pride. Egotistic leaders love crowds, but they don't like people. A true leader will have humility and compassion.

> *'But Jesus called them to Himself and said, "You know that the rulers of the Gentiles lord it over them, and those who are great exercise authority over them. Yet it shall not be so among you; but whoever **desires to become great among you, let him be your servant.**"*
> (Matthew 20:25–26)

> *'Shepherd the flock of God which is among you, serving as overseers, not by compulsion but willingly, not for dishonest gain but eagerly;* **nor as being lords over those entrusted to you, but being examples to the flock.'** (1 Peter 5:2–3)

I have listed nine situations of leadership abuse in which I have personally known the people involved. It is enlightening to recognize the pattern of control that works through these people.

1. Pulpit control

Friends of ours invited us to attend their church one Sunday. The pastor was scheduled to leave the following day for a three week mission trip out of the country. He didn't preach that day, but instead called forward every person who held a teaching or staff position in the church. He spent the entire service (well over an hour) emotionally praying for each person, prophesying over many of them, and carrying on at length. As he was doing this, it became **very** obvious what he was doing. He was establishing control. Since he was going to be out of the country (being insecure and a controller), he had to make sure he was in control even during his absence. Therefore, he went to great lengths 'reminding' everyone that he was in charge. It was revolting watching him using his manipulative tactics, especially by the fact that he was using the gifts of the Spirit to accomplish his purpose. There was absolutely no anointing present.

This man also had several manipulative family members serving in positions in the church. Board meetings were dominated by his spirit of control. Even on the tithe envelopes was a disclaimer giving him the 'authority' to use the money as he was 'led'.

2. Basically a liar

A certain pastor arrived in town promising to fulfill all the desires of a struggling church, long in need of a permanent pastor. The people, including many professionals, rejoiced that their search was finally over.

During a meeting with the core group of the church, he promised to stay for a year and conveyed a willingness to leave if things didn't work out.

Once his job became official, it only took him a few months to run the church credit card bills up to $6,000.00, spending extravagantly on multiple items for himself and the church.

When a year passed, and the church was in severe debt, one of the leaders who had originally invited him, had lunch with him. He brought up the promise regarding re-examining things in one year. The pastor replied with a defensive tone in his voice, 'You don't have that it writing.' Like many, he had no concern about the increase of the Kingdom of God; only his own financial security.

The downward spiral continued. A church member, who had already resigned from the board in disgust, received an unexpected phone call from the bank six months later, asking him what the church was going to do about their mortgage. The banker informed him that the church hadn't paid a note in six months. Appalled, and recognizing the church could bring a reproach on the city, he called his former pastor. Instead of facing reality about the finances, the pastor blatantly accused this former board member of having bitterness and unforgiveness toward him. A controller always has to sidetrack the real issue and shift the blame on the confronter. The bank was never paid, the church was reluctantly repossessed by the bank, and the empty building became a reproach. Of course, this pastor didn't have a problem, it was always someone else's fault. When he could extract no more money from the church, he resigned and now has a traveling ministry. Naturally, he doesn't tell about the irreparable damage he caused to that former church and community as he travels about, only that he served as a successful pastor.

3. *Strictly an opportunist*

In another part of the United States, a man in his mid-thirties was invited to become a pastor of a church where the previous pastor had retired. Later, as I interviewed the board members, they informed me he was a controller from the beginning. The first thing they noticed, was that upon his arrival at the city, he never came to a reception that was held for him. He was in town, but just didn't show up. He didn't apologize or explain why. This pattern continued over his two year stint. At the weekly men's prayer meetings, he would never arrive on time, and often didn't show up. The men gathering to pray would have to stand out in the parking lot, waiting for him to come and unlock the church. Often, they waited and then returned home. Again, there were no apologies or explanations. Also, he frequently would not show up for mid-week services, but have a surprise, unannounced, un-heard of guest speaker instead. No one ever knew for sure what was going on.

This is a strong characteristic of controllers – to keep you in the dark about their plans, and use the element of surprise. This keeps them in control. Of course you will never hear an apology, because they are never wrong.

This man also cunningly relocated his brother to the area, and included him in decision making, putting him on staff, etc. As his brother edged his way in, it began to irritate the church members. He wasn't the one hired, and it was unethical for him to be sharing authority.

Then the new organ, which the church had sacrificed to buy before this pastor came, was criticized. He demanded a new one, but never got it. The music store where the organ had been purchased, strongly advised that the organ not be moved around. Yet this pastor had it moved weekly, finally removing it from the auditorium and shoving it into a back storage room.

Then he began to remove pictures from the walls because he didn't like them. An artist in the church had previously painted several very tasteful and professional scenes of Christ. They were removed from the wall with no regard for her feelings. She was greatly hurt.

Typically these controllers have no diplomatic skills, and preach that no one should question their 'authority'. One cannot help questioning where the love of Christ fits in. When people are destroyed or hurt, and there is no compassion or consideration for their feelings, something is missing. Even secular businesses show more consideration for the well-being of their employees.

Things became even stranger. He callously told the congregation one Sunday that they better get used to change. Then each week without exception, plants, chairs, furniture, musical instruments, and who knows what, would be moved around or removed altogether. More and more he resorted to domination in the way he conducted himself. After all, he had to show his 'authority'.

He continually talked down his former church, elaborating on how he gave them many extra hours and was never paid overtime. He complained how that church spent money. Looking back, it was obvious that his anger was due to the fact that the money wasn't spent solely on him. The board members greatly regretted that they hadn't asked for references on the man before agreeing to his being their pastor. But as always, you expect a man of God can be trusted. We forget that Jesus said, *'Therefore by their fruits you will know them'* (Matthew 7:20).

Then money became the issue. He began to write church checks for everything, taking frequent 'ministry' trips anywhere his heart desired. The church's $20,000 savings account was rapidly depleted. Checks began to bounce. The church board had to cover bounced checks over and over again out of their own pockets. The church credit card debt went up to thousands, as he spent money like water, taking his wife to fancy dinners and making numerous other personal, but 'ministry-excused' purchases.

Worst of all, there was no flow of the spirit, only hype. The church had a history of glorious worship, but he put a stop to that, bringing in a stuffy, traditional, manipulation-ridden form of music. Songs in the spirit, were replaced by fleshly shouting and loud nerve-racking music.

Another relative moved to the area and was hired to run the sound system, and much money was spent on him, although previously the sound system was capably run by volunteers in the church.

People began to complain. No conscience. No integrity. Attendance quickly began to fade. He was confronted by the church board about his many improprieties and asked if he would consider resigning. He indicated he was willing to leave, but demanded enormous vacation pay, moving expenses and a large cash settlement. The board agreed to pay him, happy to get rid of him at any price. As one member put it, this pastor saw his position as purely a business venture anyway.

But although they met all his extreme requests, during that brief time he took a number of gullible people in the church to lunch, telling a distorted side of the story. Then he stood up on Sunday morning, and did a terrific job sounding as though he was the victim; skillfully playing on the emotions of people. He then ended the service, saying he was turning the church over to the board, and walked out the side door. Immediately, several of the families he had 'prepared' (poisoned), stood up on cue, and stomped out of the building. By the following week the 'fruit' of his ministry was even more evident. Only seven members remained in the church. The good news is that later a pastor with integrity and pure heart was hired and today the church is thriving.

4. His people, not God's

I was invited to minister to a church on a special holiday. The pastor invited another congregation from a town about one hundred miles away to join us in the weekend of celebration.

During my first session, I sensed a tremendous un-responsiveness from a number of the people.

At the next session it was the pastor's turn from the other town to preach. When he got up, the same people who didn't respond much to me, almost revered him. He was their pastor, and I sensed that in their eyes, he could do no wrong. However, it was obvious that he was keeping them captive in an inflated impression of his ability, as he projected himself as a scholar of the word, and made innuendos that all other Bible teachers knew nothing. The people ate it up, and I had the feeling that he had the people so buffaloed, that in their eyes he was more than perfect. In my own spirit, there was no edification, and the preaching was high sounding phrases, with no substance.

Looking back, I recognize that this man was a controller of people, not a man of God with a pastor's heart. To maintain a following, he had to project a sense of awe about himself. The people were nearly glassy-eyed whenever he opened his mouth to say something. When he prophesied, the words were so grandiose that there was no sense of reality.

Nearly a year later, this same pastor was approached with a dilemma by my friend, a minister I had known for years. My friend sought him out for counsel as he had a minor moral failure. He was in extreme remorse over it and wanted to do the right thing. The pastor 'counseled' him to bring the situation before the entire church and tell every detail, and then turn the church over to his elders, totally resigning his ministry. Before my friend followed this course of action, he called me, and explained the situation. Although he was willing to submit, he did not feel he had received the correct counsel.

I agreed. The counsel was from the man's head, not from the Spirit of God. Without compassion or concern, he mechanically told the man to get out of the ministry and expose the sin to the entire church (which meant the entire community). It is one thing if my friend was habitual and non-repentant in his experience, but he was not. He was extremely remorseful. As I prayed with him, I felt that the mind of the Lord was that he was to handle the situation with as few people as possible (Matthew 18:15-17) by repenting to those involved. He followed my counsel, and walked in righteousness, grateful for the grace and mercy of God. No one in his church or his city got involved, and many lives were spared the hurt and quagmire that a public confession would have caused.

Clearly, this other pastor was a controller. He had no real compassion for my friend, and desired him to lose his ministry. After all, if his ministry went down, that would make his 'unfailed' ministry look all the better. Where was love in his counsel? Love covers a multitude of sins. All he wanted to do was expose a sincerely repentant man who was supposed to be a friend.

Jezebel spirits are always hard and judgmental, mainly because it gives them a greater sense of control. You failed and I didn't. But where is the Spirit of Christ? Where is the spirit of love?

I don't condone sin in any way. But when someone truly repents, and seeks to make it right, why expose him? Why not extend mercy and cover with love? (Galatians 6:1). Why draw the entire body of Christ into a situation that will help no one and hurt many innocent people? On the other hand, if someone is habitual and unrepenting, he should be exposed (Ephesians 5:11).

5. *Abuse of authority*

Here is another case of spiritual abuse. We know of a young couple who were associate pastors under a controlling pastor.

He made unbelievable demands on them, insisting that they work long hours and never miss a board meeting. During this time they had a premature baby (born at barely over a pound) who was hospitalized off and on for four months. The baby girl was in a life-threatening situation on several occasions. When the young associate pastor asked for an occasional partial day off, the pastor always defiantly denied his request, and demanded he be at insignificant routine staff meetings instead. He always refused to change the time of the meetings, even though the young man's daughter was getting ready to undergo traumatic surgery. In fact, when the baby was a month old, the hospital called, requesting these young parents come immediately because she had contracted a yeast infection and was not expected to live through it. Our friends asked permission to leave after the worship portion of the service and make the one hour drive to the hospital. They were told absolutely not. The pastor insisted they be in the church service. The husband and wife conferred with one another, making the decision to go anyway because it involved their baby's life. The pastor finally conceded and agreed to let them go 'if you feel like you have to ... but be back tonight.'

Over the four month duration of the baby's hospitalization, the pastor only visited the hospital twice. Our friends were allowed only one day off during that four month period when the baby was critically ill.

On the two occasions that the pastor did visit the hospital, it was disastrous. This was a research hospital, and only relatives were allowed to visit at any length. When informed by the hospital staff of their brief-visitation regulations, he began making loud threats to the nurses saying he would go to the top hospital authorities. The young associates cringed at his offensiveness. They had tried to witness about the Lord to these nurses, but this pastor's inappropriate behavior left a huge black mark on the ministry. They were very embarrassed. He also stayed far beyond the allowed time frame (even for a relative) and demanded detailed information from the nurses, who were appalled at his behavior. An agreement was quickly made by the nurses and these young parents that if this pastor came to the hospital again, he was not to be allowed in under any circumstances.

This couple were also in charge of music for the church, but the pastor continually made unreasonable demands for productions, and ruled with an iron hand regarding what songs to sing in church services. Time and time again, as they sought the mind of the Holy Spirit concerning songs to sing, and ways for that part of the service to flow, they were rudely overruled by this arrogant pastor. Over and over, the pastor quickly took credit for many things this couple did behind the scenes to benefit the church. He didn't mind letting people think he was responsible for hard work his associates had performed.

Because this young man and his wife were so pure before the Lord and had the heart of servants, they endured this abuse for a two-year duration. However, finally something happened that forced them into confrontation. This young associate pastor was told by a brother-in-law of a talk that his pastor/employer had given at a pastors' conference a year previously. He was appalled at what he heard. The pastor had used the young associate and his wife as an example of certain types of personality defects. This is the point at which the couple sought me out for counsel on the matter. I encouraged them to confront the pastor.

The following day he called the pastor and confronted him about the message. The pastor confessed that he indeed did use them as an example in the talk. The young man indicated that he would like to resign immediately, having lost all respect for the man. A meeting was set up for two days later. These young associates didn't want the church damaged and for the sake of their love for the church and the people, they wanted a smooth and peaceful transition. Obviously, the pastor wanted a meeting because he feared a lawsuit for his slander.

But something incredible occurred. That evening, when these young associate pastors were in their pajamas and preparing for bed, there was a knock on the door. To their amazement, it was the pastor accompanied by a pastor of a neighboring church. Although a time had previously been agreed upon to meet the next morning, this pastor performed the act of a typical Jezebel and controlling spirit. He purposely caught them off-guard. Using this element of surprise gave him the upper hand of control, and being unprepared, their defenses would be weakened. As the young associate and his wife stood there in their bathrobes, the two pastors invited themselves in and insisted on an on-the-spot meeting. Caught entirely off guard, and reluctantly agreeing, they 'conducted' the meeting right then and there. Totally unprepared with things they had intended to bring to light, they simply agreed to resign and not press charges for the words of slander.

These young associates had no intention of a lawsuit anyway, although they were entitled to one, since their character had been maligned. They simply desired a meeting to clear the air and to state their case of all the abuses over the past two years. But the Jezebel spirit reigned again, by the element of surprise.

One of the comments this pastor flippantly made was that the secular world would never have given the young associate time off for anything. However, this young man now works for a wonderful company in another state, and has been promoted in just a few months to a prominent position that would usually take a decade to reach. God vindicated this man's excellent character. His new employer compassionately informed him that any time there is an immediate family member in the hospital, it is their policy to give as much time off as is needed (with pay).

To the dismay of an entire congregation of people who loved them, they resigned their position, choosing to protect the reputation of the church rather than dragging the matter out in front of everyone.

When this couple's home was later sold, approximately a hundred people came from the church for a farewell party. The pastor didn't come. Later, when the associate was happy attending a church in another state, this pastor called his new pastor, maligning him once again. It wasn't received.

Thank God the fruit of this former pastor's ministry

was revealed, because within a year his entire new staff resigned, unable to work with him.

6. *No God-given authority*

Concerning another situation of control, a pastor of a church where a close friend of ours attended, seemingly had no God-given authority. Therefore, he relied totally on projecting himself as an authority figure. He commonly referred to himself as the door of 'his' church, and continually reminded the people that no one had the right to question his authority.

Our friend, who was a member at his church for many years, did his best to take on the heart of a servant. Although most people recognized our friend as seasoned and having a close walk with God, this pastor never invited him to anything involving leadership. However, on one occasion they were together at a meeting of Christians, and the Lord strongly anointed our friend to minister to a visiting pastor with a great need. The way he ministered was very prophetic, and it was obvious he was under a heavy anointing. When he finished ministering, the pastor stood up and grabbed the microphone and began to brag on him in front of the group, but in such a way that clearly said, 'I'm responsible for this man's spiritual level.'

As is typical of a Jezebel spirit, he was quick to credit himself for anything positive and also would quickly separate himself from any blame for anything. Jezebels are never wrong.

He also continually surrounded himself with yes men. He would seek out those with little or no backbone, types who would rarely question his decision on any matter.

During any testimonial time, he would always thank a person, or credit the church, but would rarely thank Jesus. As a rule, Jezebels can give God credit verbally, but not from their heart. After all, they see themselves in control, and not God. They have a need for parade and show, and Jezebels (like this pastor) always have to be center stage.

Jezebels are very competitive. They hate to lose, and will not back down. Our friend shared with us that even in a Saturday afternoon game of shooting baskets, this pastor hated to lose, and would express anger and total dissatisfaction if he did lose. After all, he wasn't in control if he lost.

This pastor was very two-faced. He would strive to please both sides. Showing great favoritism, he would work hard to please everyone, but his motive was obvious, he wanted to be in total control. He frequently used flattery to win people to himself, bragging how good they were.

Toward the end of this man's tenure with this church, he became more and more rigid in everything. He began to teach from the book of Revelation, and would frequently comment, 'I don't care what anyone says, I am right.' He had studied it for several weeks, and who could possibly know more about the book of Revelation than he?

He began to seek out more education, pulling strings to take courses in nearby prestigious schools, and would then incessantly brag to people about going to those schools. It was so obvious to even his closest members that his pursuit of education was out of insecurity and not the mind of the Spirit.

A great lack of humility seems to characterize all Jezebels. After all, the spirit of control is working from a pivotal point of pride. Naturally the pride is a twisted sort, somehow birthed out of an extreme inferiority and insecurity. But nevertheless – pride.

7. *Rottenness exposed*

In another situation, a young man married the grand-daughter of the pastor of a well-established church. Recognizing a call of God on this young man's life, the pastor took him on as an associate. From the beginning the young man wanted control, actually to the point of being worshiped. He loved the praises of men and sought compliments on his intellectual capabilities continually.

When his father-in-law (who pastored along with his grandfather-in-law) had an untimely death, he went out of his way to bestow compassion and comfort to his mother-in-law.

Looking back, however, she realized that this kindness covered ulterior motives. His pattern was to always 'minister' to vulnerable people. Usually this involved women or gullible men. He always sought out the weak, and befriended only those personality types who would never disagree with him. In fact, the church often encouraged him to organize a men's retreat, but he always refused and only spent time with a few select men. He distanced himself from everyone except those whom he hand-picked.

On one occasion, he took issue with something one of the senior pastors had said. He so convincingly made his case that the other two pastors believed him. When a meeting was held, before they could jointly confront him with his grievance, he fell on his knees in front of the senior pastor, feigning a false submission and declaring his 'loyalty'. The other two pastors, who were willing to humbly confront the man, stood there in disbelief over his manipulative action to dodge the entire grievance issue.

After a few years on staff, this young associate sensed the senior pastor's grandson, and not he, would inevitably become the pastor of the church, so he began to sow seeds to destroy it. Over and over he would make comments that 'This ship is going down.' Finally he began to prophesy negative reports that the church was under judgment. But the 'prophecies' never bore witness to the senior pastor.

When the young associate was called into question on his harsh judgmental prophecies, he resigned. He claimed he could no longer be a part of a church which was in such error. But as is typical of a Jezebel spirit, he let someone else do his dirty work. His wife, whom he had so filled with his own twisted philosophies, was coerced into going to her mother (co-pastor of the church), and furiously declaring, 'From this day, you are dead to me and to my children.' Her statement broke her mother's heart, and did indeed come true, as she and the children were cut off from her for many years. Naturally, the manipulative son-in-law didn't say a word and acted shocked, although he was responsible for the entire thing. Many have tried to counsel him, but he refuses to repent and therefore, has kept a mother alienated from her daughter and grand-children for nearly a decade.

Jezebels always have someone else do their dirty work, and then stand by looking innocent, saying 'what have I done?' Yet one can seduce another person to the point (in this case, his own wife) of totally becoming a puppet in his hands, to carry out his distorted and perverted will.

Although he lived a life bent on destroying the reputa-tions of those around him, he commanded everyone else to repent. Although others challenged him to walk in forgiveness, his concept of repentance was for all others to bow down to him. As a typical controller, everyone had a need of repentance, except him.

8. A real jerk

In another situation some friends of ours encountered another Jezebel pastor. This pastor quickly proclaimed that God had called him to this certain city. People co-operated and rounded up a crowd of hungry teenagers. One veteran Christian turned over his long-time Friday night youth Bible study to him. However, instead of teach-ing the teens and imparting godliness, he got them involved in 'Christian' rock music. Within six months they were all gone, either back in the world or turned off to the things of the Lord. This pastor also caused a great deal of alarm when he emphasized deliverance meetings for the young people. Each session ended with the youth screaming violently on the floor. This filled many with fear and it was no surprise that people soon stopped coming to the church. It takes little delving into Scripture to note that Jesus **always** told the demons to be quiet. However, this pastor's ego needed to see the young people screaming (equating this 'manifestation' with spiritual results), even though absolutely no fruit ever came of it.

Things finally came to a head when the church attempted to buy a building. This pastor tried to finagle the financing with the bank to include the purchase of his own home as well. At a board meeting, he demanded that each elder co-sign for a huge loan for a church building; financing that would include his $200,000 home. When one by one concerned board members spoke up that they just couldn't jeopardize their own financial security, he stomped out of the office. Manipulation was one of his most effectual tools, loading guilt on anyone who didn't embrace his selfish plans.

A successful realtor in the church tried to explain in vain how the church was not financially able to take on this enormous endeavor. His counsel was rejected. A committed Christian attorney's counsel was also rejected. The pastor would only receive input that corresponded with what he had already planned to do. In fact, those who disagreed with his actions, would have to endure sermons conspicuously preached against them including remarks such as 'there are some who won't back the pastor,' etc.

Ultimately, this pastor successfully alienated every bank in the city, scolding them when they wouldn't grant him the loan.

This man always complained about the lack of finances that the young church had, yet nearly every day, he freely used the church funds to buy him and his friends expensive lunches. He also purchased five new cars in his two years as pastor. While the faithful congregants were struggling to keep the church afloat, he purchased a $300.00 digital phone. He was rarely in town, always off at a vitamin convention, a hunting trip, or other personal endeavors. Rarely was he at home more than two weeks of the month.

A guest evangelist ministering at his church the previous year had warned him publicly against two things: do not get into debt, and watch your pride. Those warnings were ignored as he deliberately took the church into enormous debt, and refused to submit his ego to God.

Several other characteristics reveal his abuse of a leadership position.

1. He always took people out of their strong and gifted area and put them in areas of weakness. This gave him a sense of power, making him look strong and others look weak. For example, in order to maintain power, he would take out the person gifted in music, and put a novice in his place.

2. When someone did something he liked, he used a reward system by rewarding the person with a title. However, although he awarded many titles, he was careful never to give any authority with it.

3. He would tell intimate details of people's lives, building himself up in the sight of his audience. This gave him a sense of control, as having intimate information made him look knowledgeable and powerful. He had no conscience about a minister's professional ethic of keeping things confidential.

4. Although he destroyed many lives, the closest he ever came to an apology was after an older minister rebuked him for making things complicated, and he 'apologized' to the congregation for 'speaking over their heads'. But if you are listening to God, this is not possible.

5. He consistently had to go out of town to get some personal ministry. But while the people he pastored were making financial sacrifices for him, they didn't have the means to travel themselves. Those he sought for counsel only knew one side of the story, and he could certainly make his side seem impeccable. He sought until he found, those who would valiantly take his side and tell him what he wanted to hear.

6. He had absolutely no patience. Every move was in a hurry. He didn't want anyone telling him to wait. Yet the Bible speaks often about patience! He hated

anyone questioning his ideas and would speak against such people from the pulpit. He would often make the comment that no elder was going to tell him what to do. The bottom line is that no one could tell him anything. His main agenda seemed to be to build a financial empire, at the expense of innocent and eager people who wanted to do something for God. The fruit? After spending hundreds of thousands of the hard working people's tithe money, there was not one thing to show for it, except a folded church that was a reproach to the community.

7. He was dishonest before the people and before individuals. Numerous times he announced one thing to the church body that didn't coincide with what he had told others in private. He often warned people from the pulpit against other church members who had wised up and dared to confront him.

8. This pastor continually brought up his horrible past. The implication was clear, 'Any way you name it, I'm cool.' He boasted about his past life, his way with women, his physical toughness, etc. What does this have to do with the Kingdom of God? Love? A servant's heart? It sounded more like a macho image imbedded in insecurity that couldn't get enough recognition and attention.

9. He insisted that people confess their sin before the entire body. He acted as a hard judge graphically implying, 'You sinned, and I didn't. I'm strong and you're not.' This gave him a sense of power, and the upper hand. He spoke as a brutal judge without compassion – wanting all sin exposed, not covered. Yet he would constantly use the term, as he spoke to his own people who would question things, 'You're not covering my nakedness.'

Potentially he could have had a thriving church and added many souls to the Kingdom, but he was eclipsed by his own ego. Everyone else needed repentance, except him. He was accountable to no one.

Conclusion? Beware of anyone who is never wrong.

The fruit of his ministry? The entire church disbanded. He is no longer there, but off in another city, repeating the same scenario. The former church members tried to warn the leaders to whom he freshly submitted himself. However, the new group was too excited about his being a part of their organization to listen. They'll learn the hard way. It's hard to imagine how many souls will be eternally wounded in the process. Maybe some day this 'leader' will be able to receive correction from God.

9. People would rather be coerced than led

In yet another situation, a friend of ours accepted a pastorate of a three-hundred member church. The church thrived under his preaching at first, until the Spirit began to move against their tradition. The old wine skins had no tolerance or desire for anything fresh from the Spirit. As this anointed and gifted man tried to yield to the purposes of God, he found himself being opposed. Soon there was a rumor started against him, and a committee was formed to vote him out. The politicking was unbelievable, with people putting in their votes two and three times. One man even had his invalid mother, who hadn't been in the church for a year, vote. Her mental condition disabled her to even know what she was doing.

Upon his leaving, our friend spoke frankly to the committee concerning a man they were seeking to replace him. 'This man is going to do to you what you did to me.' Soon after this new pastor was installed, he began to **take** from the church financially and caused great division. When he finally resigned from the church which eventually saw through his tactics, the real damage had been done.

It reminds one of the warnings God spoke to Israel when they desired a king like the other nations had.

> *'So Samuel told all the words of the Lord to the people who asked him for a king. And he said, "This will be the*

behavior of the king who will reign over you: He will **take** *your sons and appoint them for his own chariots and to be his horsemen ... He will* **take** *your daughters to be his perfumers, cooks and bakers. And he will* **take** *the best of your fields, your vineyards, and your olive groves, and give them to his servants. He will* **take** *a tenth of your grain and your vintage, and give it to his officers and servants. He will* **take** *your male servants, your female servants, your finest young men, and your donkeys, and put them to his work. He will* **take** *a tenth of your sheep. And you will be his servants." '*

(1 Samuel 8:10–17)

The new pastor went from house to house, taking people aside, picking those naive enough to somehow believe that the church had ripped him off. Increasingly he gained sympathy until he had a favorable following. The same people who wouldn't stand with our friend for legitimate reasons, now stood with this man who was totally functioning under a Jezebel spirit.

Our friend a year previously had moved to another town and started a new work from scratch. The people who had claimed loyalty to him, but didn't stand for him when he was persecuted by this denomination, now followed this recently expelled Jezebel pastor. Where do you suppose he started a church? In the same town that our friend did, where he blatantly began to compete with him.

But people would rather be coerced than led. Our friend had a pure motive to start a church that could experience pure worship with the Holy Spirit in control. Although the former church people saw it, they weren't strong enough to shake the denominational ties; yet they now were extremely loyal to a Jezebel. Our friend had tried to lead them the way of the Spirit. They wouldn't go. But when the Jezebel coerced them, they followed him. Now, three years later, those once so appreciative of our friend's message have never darkened the door of his new church.

It becomes more incredible. This Jezebel pastor continually sows bad seed against my friend. When my friend has a guest minister in, he finds out the dates and then invites a guest in for the very same dates.

Our friend had a tremendously successful tent meeting his first summer in the city. The next year he planned it again. To his amazement, this Jezebel pastor also planned a tent meeting, during the same dates. The third year, he again planned a tent meeting on the same dates as our friend, although the dates were set a year in advance.

Insecurity is rampant in this Jezebel pastor! He is extremely possessive of his people, and he can't bear not to be in competition with our friend, for fear of losing his people. The coerced people continue to believe every lie, and follow him loyally. People today, as Israel once was, would rather be coerced than led.

God wants to lead His people personally. When will we learn?

It seems apparent that we would still rather have man tell us a lie than to take the trouble to go to God for the truth.

> *'None of them shall teach his neighbor, and none his brother, saying, "Know the Lord," **for all shall know Me, from the least of them to the greatest of them.'***
>
> (Hebrews 8:11)

Chapter 9

You Can Live Higher

- God is always on my mind.

The Holy Spirit provides a way for us to live in a higher realm.

One afternoon, as I was sitting on our deck, my attention was drawn to our cat. As always, it would spend time in the back of the house stalking birds. I watched the little sparrow run ahead a few feet as our large gray cat stalked it. Suddenly, just when the cat was ready to pounce, the bird seemed to receive a revelation. The bird realized it had two dimensions. It not only could walk, but it could also fly. Instantly it took off, leaving the earthbound realm, where the cat was destined to stay. As it gracefully and confidently flew away, it was as if it was saying, 'See you later Mr Cat.'

Christians can live in a higher dimension. We have to decide as individuals if we are going to live in an earthbound realm, forever defeated and stalked by the enemy (seeking whom he may devour), or if we are going to live in a higher dimension of God, the realm of the Holy Spirit, which He has made available for each of us.

The realm of the Holy Spirit is accessible to every believer, although few seem to take advantage of it.

Through the Person of the Holy Spirit we can live above circumstances, the cares of this world, and avoid succumbing to defeat, distractions, depression and discouragement.

Encourage Yourself!

David was an example of this. At Ziklag, the enemy had taken everything.

> *'So David and his men came to the city, and there it was, burned with fire; and their wives, their sons, and their daughters had been taken captive.'*
>
> (1 Samuel 30:3)

It would have been easy for David to kick himself, and indulge in self-pity, sliding into an all-time low of depression. But David was a man who chose to live higher!

Many were against him, but he chose to rise up in the Spirit.

> *'Now David was greatly distressed, for the people spoke of stoning him, because the soul of all the people was grieved, every man for his sons and his daughters.* **But David strengthened (encouraged) himself in the Lord his God.'** (1 Samuel 30:6)

After David encouraged himself, he asked Abiathar the priest to bring him the ephod.

> *'So **David inquired of the Lord**, saying, "Shall I pursue this troop? Shall I overtake them?" And He answered him,* **"Pursue, for you shall surely overtake them and without fail recover all."** *'* (1 Samuel 30:8)

It is interesting that pursuing the enemy was not even on the people's minds. They had already conceded defeat and had made David their scapegoat. But the Lord fulfilled His word to David.

> *'So David recovered all that the Amalekites had carried*
> *away, and David rescued his two wives. And **nothing of***
> ***theirs was lacking**, either small or great, sons or daugh-*
> *ters, spoil or anything which they had taken from them;*
> ***David recovered all.'*** (1 Samuel 30:18–19)

But there would have been no victory if David hadn't **chosen** to encourage himself in the Lord.

God has good news for His people, but we **miss hearing it** if we don't choose to rise up in the realm of the Spirit and seek His mind. His way is always available to us, but we must choose the Spirit and resist staying earthbound in the flesh. Depressed people always see and hear in distortion. Depression is a built-in disclaimer to any good or triumphant facts that God has to proclaim.

What Hinders Us From Living Higher?

Two things predominately keep believers from reaching a higher realm in God; self-satisfaction and distractions.

Self-satisfaction ties the hands of God. God responds to the hungry, the desperate, the needy, but He can do nothing for those who are content where they are. Some whom God has greatly blessed, have slid into mediocrity, no longer seeking Him.

Distractions look important, but abort all opportunities of pursuing God and experiencing what He has. This is probably one of the most powerful and effective tools of the devil, and we need to be on guard against every form of diversion. It is easy to become distracted with things that appear to have importance, but in reality they amount to little. Jesus spoke to Martha who was in strife as she prepared in the kitchen,

> *'Martha, Martha, you are worried and troubled*
> *(distracted) about many things, but **one thing is***
> ***needed**, and Mary has chosen the good part, which will*
> *not be taken away from her.'* (Luke 10:41–42)

The implication is that Mary ***will have for eternity*** what she is receiving from Jesus as she sits at his feet.

How quickly we sell ourselves out to the demands of endless distractions, much of which will be taken from us, although we spend immeasurable time at them.

> *'Each one's work will become clear: for the Day will declare it, because it will be revealed by fire; and the fire will test each one's work, of what sort it is. If anyone's work which he has built on it **endures**, he will receive a reward.'*   (1 Corinthians 3:13–14)

God's Only Limitation

God is certainly not limited by the devil. The only thing that limits God is the limitation put upon Him by man.

God is a big thinker. He doesn't just answer prayer, He always gives far beyond what we ask or think. *'Now to Him who is able to do **exceedingly, abundantly above** all that we **ask or think**, according to the power that works in us'* (Ephesians 3:20).

He doesn't just forgive, He forgives abundantly. *'. . . Let him return to the Lord, and He will have mercy on him; and to our God, for He will **abundantly pardon**'* (Isaiah 55:7).

God doesn't just extend mercy, He abounds in mercy. *'The Lord is merciful and gracious, slow to anger, and **abounding in mercy**'* (Psalm 103:8).

He doesn't just bless, He loads us! *'Blessed be the Lord, Who **daily loads us with benefits**'* (Psalm 68:19).

He not only fulfills, but brings us to rich fulfillment. *'. . . We went through fire and water, but You brought us out to **rich fulfillment**'* (Psalm 66:12).

He's the God of abundance! *'The river of God is **full** of water'* (Psalm 65:9).

Jesus expressed His frustration with small thinking as He rebuked the disciples. When Jesus told them to beware of the leaven (doctrine) of the scribes and the Pharisees, the disciples in their carnality thought he was reprimanding them for not bringing bread with them.

> '"When I broke the five loaves for the five thousand, how many baskets **full of fragments did you have left over**?" They said to Him, "Twelve."
>
> "Also, when I broke the seven for the four thousand, how many **large baskets full of fragments did you take up**?" And they said, "Seven."
>
> So He said to them, "How is it you do not understand?"'
>
> (Mark 8:19–21)

Notice how specifically He speaks – five loaves for five thousand and twelve full baskets left over. And seven loaves for four thousand and seven large full baskets left over.

He was explaining that He was the God of abundance and was disappointed at their small thinking. They were worried about the supply of bread. He was saying, I not only can create bread, but when I do, I have a huge (large full baskets) supply left over.

God not only answers prayer, He has trouble putting the brakes on! How long will we limit Him? When we pray we need to pray with large expectation. Rather than asking God to fill our thimble, we need to ask Him to fill our dumptruck. He is the God of the impossible! It's time to believe the Gospel.

When we pray we also need to remember that He **qualified us!**

> 'Giving thanks to the Father who has **qualified us** to be partakers of the inheritance of the saints in the light.'
>
> (Colossians 1:12)

Also that He freely gives us all things.

> *'He who did not spare His own Son, but delivered Him up for us all, how shall He not with Him also **freely give us all things**.'*
> (Romans 8:32)

Additionally, let's not forget that God has made a final decision concerning all His promises to us.

> *'For **all the promises** of God in Him are Yes, and in Him Amen, to the glory of God through us.'*
> (2 Corinthians 1:20)

Get into the Spirit!

When five kings found themselves in a desperate situation, not having water for the army or the animals that followed them, the King of Israel spoke an evil report.

> *'And the king of Israel said, Alas! For the Lord has called these three kings together to deliver them into the hand of Moab.'*
> (2 Kings 3:10)

It is amazing how some people speak and react the minute something goes wrong. They not only profess that we're defeated, but that God did it to us. But thank God for a man who chose to **live higher** in spite of circumstances. He answered this evil report by a question. He reached for God.

> *'But Jehoshaphat said, "Is there no prophet of the Lord here, that we may inquire of the Lord by him?" So one of the servants of the king of Israel answered and said, "Elisha the son of Shaphat is here, who poured water on the hands of Elijah."'*
> (2 Kings 3:11)

When they came to Elisha, he wasn't overjoyed to see them. He was angry at the way that these people had a history of turning to false prophets.

> 'Then Elisha said to the king of Israel, "What have I to do with you? Go to the prophets of your father and the prophets of your mother..."
>
> And Elisha said, "As the Lord of hosts lives, before whom I stand, surely were it not that I regard the presence of Jehoshaphat king of Judah, I would not look at you, nor see you."' (2 Kings 3:13–14)

Elisha was angry, and had no interest in helping them, except for the reputation of Jehoshaphat. **Elisha had to get in the Spirit!**

Like many people who were once used of God, Elisha became cynical. Because of the disappointment leaders experience when people abort the potential to which God has called them, often they become sarcastic and cynical. So Elisha had to rise into the Spirit. He had to begin to worship, in order to ascend into the realm of the Spirit. As he worshiped, the Lord spoke.

> '"But now bring me a musician." Then it happened, when the musician played, that the **hand of the Lord came upon him**. And he said, "Make this valley full of ditches. For thus says the Lord: 'You shall not see wind, nor shall you see rain; yet that valley shall be filled with water, so that you, your cattle, and your animals may drink. And this is a simple matter in the sight of the Lord...'"' (2 Kings 3:15–18)

The word of the Lord came when Elisha made a decision to get in the Spirit, by calling a musician to play.

How many times does God have a word for us, if we choose to rise up in the Spirit? No doubt all the time! But if we choose to stay angry, or disappointed, or frustrated, it will keep us from living higher and soaring above circumstances.

We Don't Have the Luxury of Looking at the Natural

God's ways are higher than man's ways (Isaiah 55:9). Therefore, when God speaks to us by His Spirit, there may not be 'proof' or evidence to satisfy our eyes and ears. But we know that God sees from a higher perspective, and we have to choose to believe Him, and not trust our natural senses. It seems that whenever God speaks to us, the natural surroundings seem to contradict what He is saying. But God calls things that are not, as though they already exist (Romans 4:17). A weatherman will tell you on a sunny day that it is going to rain. He has access to equipment that gives him this knowledge, so we believe him. Equally, we believe the report of the Lord. He cannot lie. *'For all the promises of God in Him are Yes, and in Him Amen, to the glory of God through us'* (2 Corinthians 1:20).

Don't Give in to Passivity

One of the greatest weaknesses I've seen among believers is that of giving into passivity. Passivity frustrates the grace of God because faith always works in tension. No athlete would enjoy competing against a team who wasn't trying or who forfeited the game. The opposition is what makes competition exciting. We must be willing to fight. For example, in prayer there are times when you just can't seem to break through. In your spirit you know you haven't reached the place of satisfaction and the knowledge that you have touched God. That is the time to press in with diligence and not let up. You just assume God is not hearing you, but those are the times you are being resisted. So it is important to fight, and remain in an aggressive posture.

The angel told Daniel after he had prayed 21 days, *'Do not fear, Daniel, for from the first day that you set your heart to understand, and to humble yourself before* *your God, **your words were heard**; and I have come because of your words. But the prince of the kingdom of Persia withstood me twenty one days . . . '* (Daniel 10:12–13).

The Baptism in the Holy Spirit

The exciting thing about the baptism in the Holy Spirit is the aspect of living in a higher realm with God.

The prayer language (speaking in tongues) is a realm of prayer that is higher than the natural range of prayer.

> *'For he who speaks in a tongue does not speak to men but to God, for no one understands him; however, in the spirit he speaks mysteries.'*   (1 Corinthians 14:2)

When a believer prays in tongues, he is bypassing the limitations of his brain, and speaking to God in the Spirit. In fact, it is the same with all the gifts of the Spirit – prophecy, word of knowledge, word of wisdom, etc. No manifestation of the Spirit is a product of the brain, but rather a gift and manifestation of the Holy Spirit.

What awesome news it is that when we pray in the Spirit, we are bypassing our minds and praying perfectly, and according to the will of God! Some complain that they don't want to pray what they don't understand. But the prayer language is the one gift our brain cannot defile, because we don't understand it.

> *'Likewise the Spirit also helps in our weaknesses. For we do not know what we should pray for as we ought, but the Spirit Himself makes intercession for us with groanings which cannot be uttered. Now He who searches the hearts knows what the mind of the Spirit is, because He makes intercession for the saints **according to the will of God.'***   (Romans 8:26–27)

The baptism in the Holy Spirit with the evidence of tongues and the gifts of the Spirit, is not an end, but a beginning – a threshold! Having this experience doesn't guarantee maturity any more than saying wedding vows guarantees a good marriage. Results and maturity come when we choose to follow the Spirit, yield to His voice and let Him work in our lives.

Through the Spirit, we can minister the gifts of the Holy Spirit. We can **live higher** by putting to death the deeds of the flesh.

> *'For if you live according to the flesh you will die; but if* ***by the Spirit*** *you put to death the deeds of the body, you will live.'*   (Romans 8:13)

Through the Spirit we can put to death the habits of the flesh, and overcome all areas that have defeated us in the past. Through the Spirit we can live above depression and heaviness, overcome addictions and live a godly lifestyle.

Our Responsibility

This is where most people miss it. They are waiting for the Lord to come down and do something for them. But God waits for us to choose to rise into the realm of the Spirit.

For example, when you enter a church service, you may not feel like singing and worshiping. Yet you choose to enter in. Soon you experience the presence of the Lord, and troubles and worries you were experiencing previously fade in their magnitude. You have entered a higher realm.

Paul had to exhort Timothy to stir up the Holy Spirit within him.

> *'Therefore I remind you to* ***stir up the gift of God*** *which is in you through the laying on of my hands. For God has not given us a spirit of fear, but of power and of love and of a sound mind.'*   (2 Timothy 1:6–7)

God is always available, but He must be pursued – He must be sought. The Holy Spirit within the believer has a wonderful ability to be stirred up. If we don't stir up His presence, He will remain dormant, and His awesome power will not be utilized in our behalf.

The sun is shining every day. Naturally, many days the clouds are in the way. But if you board a commercial jet on even the most cloudy day, you will fly above the clouds and experience total sunshine. Through the Holy Spirit we can fly above the circumstances and obstacles. But we have to choose to fly with Him. If we are willing, He is willing.

Know No One After the Flesh

One problem we all have is remembering the exhortation from the Lord that we are not to know one another after the flesh.

> *'Therefore, from now on, we regard no one according to the flesh. Even though we have known Christ according to the flesh, yet now we know Him thus no longer.'*
> (2 Corinthians 5:16)

By the grace of God, we can look beyond human flesh, strengths and weaknesses, personalities, and accomplishments and behold the Christ in one another. Our flesh is capable of nothing. My flesh can't help you, and your flesh can't help me; but the Holy Spirit within each other can contribute great things.

Even our fellowship is to be in the Spirit. There is nothing wrong with sharing common interests, but we have to choose to **live higher** by going beyond the soulish fellowship and fellowshiping by the Spirit. Some Christians just live in the soul realm. They don't talk about the things of God, pray fervently, and seldom read their Bibles. Although they have placed their faith in God, they don't live accordingly. Soulish people don't cultivate fellowship with the Holy Spirit. Their inner man stays earthbound.

Knowing one another after the flesh causes us to miss what God has for us. What a travesty it was when Jesus was in His own home town, and although He had much to give, they looked through the eyes of the flesh and couldn't recognize Him as sent from God.

> '... *And many hearing Him were astonished, saying, "Where did this Man get these things? And what wisdom is this which is given to Him, that such mighty works are performed by His hands!* **Is this not the carpenter, the Son of Mary, and brother of James, Joses, Judas, and Simon? And are not His sisters here with us?" And they were offended at Him.**'
>
> (Mark 6:2–3)

> '*Now he* **could do no mighty work there**, *except that He laid His hands on a few sick people and healed them. And He* **marveled because of their unbelief**.'
>
> (Mark 6:5–6)

Looking at one another through natural eyes will simply rob us from receiving from God. The person of whom we may be critical, may be the very vessel that God desires to use to speak into our lives.

There are many extraordinary manifestations of the Holy Spirit going on all over the world. The wind of the Holy Spirit is blowing in unprecedented ways. We must be careful not to look at what is happening to individuals through critical eyes. We must choose to look through the eyes of the Spirit.

As the Spirit moves, will some people get in the flesh? Yes, but be careful to avoid seeing anyone through a critical eye. If we judge through the flesh, we may be criticizing God.

When the ark of the Lord was being brought into the city of David, David was obviously making praise in a most exuberant manner.

> '*As the ark of the Lord came into the City of David, Michal, Saul's daughter, looked through a window and* **saw King David leaping and whirling before the Lord; and she despised him in her heart**.'   (2 Samuel 6:16)

Michal mocked David for his behavior.

> '*. . . And Michal the daughter of Saul came out to meet David, and said, "How glorious was the king of Israel today, uncovering himself today in the eyes of the maids of his servants, as one of the base fellows shamelessly uncovers himself!"*'   (2 Samuel 6:20)

David's response should serve a warning for us.

> '*So David said to Michal, "It was before the Lord, who chose me instead of your father and all his house, to appoint me ruler over the people of the Lord, over Israel.* **Therefore I will play music before the Lord. And I will be even more undignified than this, and will be humble in my own sight. But as for the maidservants of whom you have spoken, by them I will be held in honor**." *Therefore Michal the daughter of Saul* **had no children to the day of her death**.'   (2 Samuel 6:21–23)

Don't Judge by Outward Appearance

One of the greatest disciplines we can gain as believers is to refuse to judge by outward appearance, and **choose** to look through the eyes of the Spirit.

Michal looked through the window, which represented looking through her natural eyes. She refused to recognize that David was enthralled with the presence of God, and was dancing before Him with all his might. Because of her carnality, she couldn't see him in pure worship. Instead she accused him out of a jealous heart of being uncovered before the maidservants.

David retorted with righteous indignation. She was speaking against his relationship with God. He declared he would be even more undignified (as unto God) and proclaimed that even these maidservants would recognize his devotion to the Lord (which she couldn't see) and they would hold him in honor for it.

Personally, every time I judge something without consulting the Lord, I'm wrong. May God give each of us the grace to desire to look through His eyes.

God had to correct Samuel, because he was looking through his natural eyes. He desired to anoint Eliab, who looked good on the outside, but was rotten on the inside. Samuel was impressed, saying, *'Surely the Lord's anointed is before Him'* (1 Samuel 16:6). But God had to remind him not to judge by outward appearance.

> *'Do not look at his appearance or at his physical stature, because I have refused him.* **For the Lord does not see as man sees; for man looks at the outward appearance, but the Lord looks at the heart.** *'*
>
> (1 Samuel 16:7)

So often the church has been guilty of judging from the outward appearance. Just as Samuel began to judge by his own eyes, saying *'Surely the Lord's anointed is before Him.'* What we judge as good, is only an outward appearance, and we fail to see that the inside is rotten to the core. It was Eliab who resisted David, when David was on a mission to kill Goliath. Eliab was so full of jealousy and pride that when David began asking questions, and saying *'Who is this uncircumcised Philistine, that should defy the armies of the living God?'* Eliab accused him angrily and wrongly.

> *'Now Eliab his oldest brother heard when he spoke to the men; and Eliab's anger was aroused against David, and he said, "Why did you come down here? And with whom have you left those few sheep in the wilderness? I*

> **know your pride and the insolence of your heart**, *for you have come down here to see the battle."* '
>
> (1 Samuel 17:28)

Eliab was full of baloney. He was accusing David of the wickedness that was in his own heart, not David's. How long have we revered those in the church who look good on the outside, but are carnal and jealous and full of pride on the inside? Because they have an impressive stature or an eloquence of speech, we equate that to spirituality. We end up with men pleasing men and the Holy Spirit is left out of the picture. Too many churches are built on the pastor's personality instead of leaders who are letting God take control.

It's Not How You Start – It's How You Finish

The body of Christ is learning that we can live in the Spirit at all times. *'If we live in the Spirit, let us also walk in the Spirit'* (Galatians 5:25). God is glorified as we walk in the Spirit.

Early one morning, the Lord spoke the words to me, 'It's not how you start – it's how you finish.'

As I've meditated upon these words, it has become obvious that God is more interested in how we finish our life than how we began it. Just like a race, it doesn't matter how wonderful a beginning you had; what counts is crossing the finish line first. When you cross the finish line, no one cares if you had a good start or a bad start of the race – only that you won.

Many have begun their Christian life with a mighty splash and served God with zeal. However, some of those same people have let their zeal regress into lukewarmness, and mediocrity. These are days to plug into God and seek His face for the vision and purpose He has for us as individuals. There is no greater experience than to live a life that fulfills God's purpose.

'. . .I have found David the son of Jesse, a man after My own heart, who will do (fulfill) *all My will.'*

(Acts 13:22)

Chapter 10

Going to the Other Side

*'Let us cross over to the **other side** of the Lake.'*
(Luke 8:22)

One thing few people seem to understand is that God desires to promote people. As long as we are choosing to follow Him with our entire hearts, He intends to advance us and promote us. Naturally the rate of promotion has to do with humility, the attitude of our hearts, and our willingness to let God correct us. His desire is that, in the entirety of our Christian walk, we experience perpetual growth, just as parents expect to see their children grow and mature.

How Far Will You Let God Take You?

Overall, the question that God proposes to us is how far we will let Him perfect or mature us. After all, His purpose is to conform us to the image of His own Son. *'For whom He foreknew, He also predestined to be conformed to the image of His Son, that He might be the firstborn among many brethren'* (Romans 8:29).

To every believer, God desires to manifest ultimate maturity in Christ. However, maturity is a process, and many choose not to yield to His correcting hand.

God Promoted Peter

Throughout the New Testament, Jesus gave Peter little slack, frequently correcting him.

For example, when Peter was the only disciple willing to get out of the boat during the storm, and successfully walk on water, Jesus didn't congratulate him. He said, *'O you of little faith, why did you doubt?'* (Matthew 14:31). Those were strong words for a man who had just walked on water.

When Peter tried to 'comfort' Jesus by rebuking His words that He would be crucified, Jesus spoke scathingly to him, *'Get behind Me, Satan! You are an offense to Me, for you are not mindful of the things of God, but the things of men'* (Matthew 16:23).

When Peter questioned the Lord about forgiving his brother, Jesus told him, *'I do not say to you, up to seven times, but up to seventy times seven'* (Matthew 18:22).

Jesus told Peter that He would deny Him three times (Matthew 26).

Jesus questioned Peter in the garden of Gethsemane, *'What, could you not watch with Me one hour?'* (Matthew 26:40).

Three times Jesus questioned Peter, *'Do you love Me?'* (John 21:15–17).

When God Corrects Us, He Does it with a Sense of Destiny!

Sometimes we reject God's correcting hand, somehow thinking that God is trying to withhold from us or keep us from some pleasure we desire. But the Scripture plainly says that the Lord corrects the sons He loves (Hebrews 12:6). And if we receive correction, then promotion follows.

So, although Jesus spoke strongly to Peter, His corrections to him were all given with a sense of destiny. God had promotion in mind!

149

After Jesus' resurrection, an angel gave orders to Mary Magdalene, and to Mary, the mother of James, and Salome to *'Go and tell His disciples – **and Peter** – that He is going before you into Galilee; there you will see Him, as He said to you'* (Mark 16:7). The angel put special emphasis on Peter's name.

Again, it was Peter, whom the Holy Spirit used as the keynote speaker on the day of Pentecost. *'But Peter, standing up with the eleven . . . '* (Acts 2:14–40).

And talk about promotion, it was Peter whose shadow passing over people caused them to be healed. *'So that they brought the sick out into the streets and laid them on beds and couches, that at least the **shadow of Peter** passing by might fall on some of them'* (Acts 5:15).

God takes us to maturity, so that the very shadow of our life begins to touch everyone we come in contact with. More miracles were attributed to Peter's ministry than to any other disciple.

A large part of the process of growing spiritually is not only that we are learning to trust God, but that God is able to trust us with more responsibility. For example, even though you love a small child, you cannot trust him to drive the car. Equally, God's loving us does not necessarily mean that He can trust us.

Paul's words to the Corinthian church ring with such truth.

> *'When I was a child, I spoke as a child, I understood as a child, I thought as a child; but when I became a man, I put away childish things.'* (1 Corinthians 13:11)

As long as we are willing and obedient (see Isaiah 1:19) we will see increase, and experience the best that God has.

Going to the Other Side

As Christians, we are, in effect, always in a process of

going to the other side. In fact, from the very day we were born again we were translated to the other side.

> *'He has delivered us from the power of darkness and translated us into the Kingdom of the Son of His love.'*
> (Colossians 1:13)

At one point Jesus gave a command to His disciples to go to the other side of the lake. *'"Let us go over to the **other side** of the lake." And they launched out'* (Luke 8:22).

But as they began to sail, He fell asleep. Then a windstorm came up; the boat began to fill with water and they were in danger.

In the middle of this they woke up Jesus, saying, *'Master, Master, we are perishing!'* (Luke 8:24). So Jesus rose up and rebuked the wind and the raging of the water, and everything became calm.

Then He rebuked them, saying, *'Where is your faith?'* (Luke 8:25).

Jesus meant what He said when He gave the command to depart to the other side.

Storms, giants, and all other obstacles are irrelevant when God speaks to us. Jesus didn't prophesy that they would encounter a storm, He only gave the command to go to the other side.

When God commanded that spies be sent in to check out the promised land (Numbers 13), He didn't mention that there were giants in the land. God doesn't mention storms and giants because they are irrelevant to Him. Hindrances, resistance, obstacles and other extraneous circumstances are only things to overcome in the process that will make us stronger. Speaking to storms, fighting giants, and resisting hindrances, increase our faith and develop spiritual muscles. No one can become strong merely watching someone else exercise.

The bottom line is that God is taking us to the other side! The end result is that we are changed. We are different. The disciples were not only geographically in a different location, but their inner man was transformed. No doubt they experienced a peace in future storms they had never known. They had an indescribable substantive peace any time they set foot on a boat.

When we go through a storm, God deposits something in us that wasn't there before. He adds a dimension of Himself to our lives.

Peter Went to the Other Side

A statement Jesus made to Peter seems almost perplexing at first. He says, *'Simon, Simon! Indeed, Satan has asked for you, that he may sift you as wheat. But I have prayed for you, that your faith should not fail; and when you have returned to Me, strengthen your brethren'* (Luke 22:31–32).

To the natural mind, you would expect Jesus to say that He had rebuked Satan and commanded him to leave Peter alone. Instead, He only promises to pray for him.

However, in the promise to pray is also a promise that he will be taken to the other side! Jesus had said, *'When you have returned to Me, strengthen your brethren.'* Jesus didn't say, '**If** you return to Me' but '**When** you return to Me.' He had confidence that His prayers for Peter would be answered, and that they would work so well, so completely, that Peter would be taken to the other side – changed. So changed would he be that he would be able to strengthen his brothers. Whenever God takes us somewhere, He always changes us in the process.

God is always concerned with what is coming out of us. Rather than merely existing as Christians, He wants virtue flowing out of us. You can't go to the other side without **receiving** from God that which will be a strength to someone else.

God brings us to the other side, to higher realms of maturity, in order that substance and virtue will flow from us to minister to those in need.

The End of Self is the Beginning of God

> *'Then He said, "I tell you, Peter, the rooster shall not crow this day before you will deny **three times** that you know Me.'* (Luke 22:34)

Peter did just as Jesus said. He denied him three times, including angrily denying his association with Him to a servant girl (Luke 22:57). To the natural mind, it seems that Peter totally failed God. Luke says, *'The Lord turned and looked at Peter'* (Luke 22:61). The look unquestionably was of one of compassion, however, and not accusation.

What we call failure, God doesn't necessarily call failure. Sometimes the best thing that can happen is that we come to the end of ourselves. The end of self is the beginning of God! Sometimes it takes us years to admit we **can't** do something, but when we admit our helplessness, God immediately takes us to the other side.

In the power of our flesh we cannot please God (Romans 8:8). Only through the power of the Spirit can we truly overcome.

> *'For if you live according to the flesh you will die; but if by the Spirit you put to death the deeds of the body, you will live.'* (Romans 8:13)

Pride says, 'If I just try a little harder,' but humility says, 'I can only do it through the power of the Spirit.' Sometimes it takes us years to recognize that the New Covenant has nothing to do with performance, but rather just responding to God. This is where most people have a problem. Our flesh wants to perform. Many Christians are still tied to performance. They are trying to get God to accept them for their good works. But the New Covenant isn't works, rather it is faith in His **finished work**. *'It is finished'* (John 19:30). We want part of the credit. It frustrates our flesh to have to depend totally on God. He requires no performance, only obedience and response.

We're All Gonna Die!

There are some people who almost thrive on things going wrong. They live as though they've been anticipating and expecting trouble. Then when struggles arise, they immediately yield to hopelessness and proclaim in so many words, 'We're all going to die.'

Hating bondage is not enough. We must desire God. God doesn't just deliver us from sin and bondage, but **delivers us into** righteousness and freedom. It is not enough to stop sinning, but we must be caught up in God's presence and enjoy Him.

The children of Israel had a vision to get out of Egypt, but they lacked a vision to go on with God; that is to go into the promised land. When God delivers us, we need not only a vision to come out, but also a vision to go in! If we don't have a vision to go in (to the promises of God), fear will paralyze us when we are confronted with obstacles or opposition.

When Moses brought Israel out of Egypt, the Scripture says that,

> *'God did not lead them by the way of the land of the Philistines, although that was near; for God said, "**Lest perhaps the people change their minds when they see war, and return to Egypt.**"'* (Exodus 13:17)

God knows our failings. We are not fighters by nature. No wonder Paul said, *'In my flesh dwells no good thing.'* God hemmed in the Israelites, so they couldn't retreat. They had mountains on both sides, the Red Sea in front of them, and Pharaoh and his army in close pursuit.

First the children of Israel cried out to the Lord – then to Moses.

> *'Because there were no graves in Egypt, have you taken us away to die in the wilderness? Why have you dealt with us, to bring us up out of Egypt?'* (Exodus 14:11)

Notice the sarcasm in their voices. Some people perpetually speak in this manner no matter what God has done for them. Imagine what they've just seen God do for them. He had taken them out from 400 years of bondage with Pharaoh, He moved on the Egyptians to lavish them with gold (400 years of back pay), yet their hearts were still hardened.

The sarcasm was declaring God's inability to deliver them. They were saying, in effect, that since there weren't large enough cemeteries in Egypt, they had been brought out to be killed and buried in the desert.

A popular commercial states, 'You can take the boy out of the country, but you can't take the country out of the boy.' I've heard preachers say, 'God took only a few days to get them out of Egypt, but it took Him forty years to get the Egypt out of them.'

You can always tell where people are, spiritually speaking, by the whine (or lack of whine) in their voices. Some just never stop whining. God won't do much until the whining stops and turns into praise.

Conflict Means You Are Going to the Other Side

It seems we whine the loudest right before God takes us to ultimate victory. Listen to Moses,

> *'And Moses said to the people, "Do not be afraid. Stand still, and see the salvation of the Lord, which He will accomplish for you today. For the Egyptians whom you see today, **you shall see again no more forever**. The Lord will fight for you, and you shall hold your peace.'*
> (Exodus 14:13–14)

155

What a declaration! *'The Egyptians whom you see today, you shall see again no more forever.'*

The very thing that followed them and held them in bondage was going to be buried forever! What is your greatest weakness? What is that thing that follows your life? Right here in the midst of conflict, God is going to take you to the other side, and bury that old thing in the process; your main problem (Pharaoh) and all the problems (the army) that goes along with it.

The Narrow Gate Squeezes You into Life

Before every victory, there is a conflict. If not, we couldn't call it victory.

A much overlooked Scripture has awesome meaning.

> *'Enter by the **narrow gate**; for wide is the gate and broad is the way that leads to destruction, and there are many who go in by it. Because narrow is the gate and **difficult** is the way which leads to life, and there are few who find it.'* (Matthew 7:13–14)

When God led Moses and the children of Israel out of Egypt, they stood at the Red Sea, with no possible means of escape. They were at the narrow gate. The Egyptian army was closing in on them, and mountains surrounded them on both sides. The narrow gate is the way to life. It lets us pass to the other side. The word 'narrow' means confined.

It is in that confined place that we have to trust God. Going through the narrow place will squeeze out unbelief and all fleshly effort. Jesus said, *'Wide is the gate and broad is the way that leads to destruction...'* Multitudes choose the broad way, the way with no conflict, no confrontation. They only want comfort and convenience.

Those are the people who are fine as long as things are smooth, but the minute something goes wrong they can only see the negative. God desires to change their negative hearts and plug them into positive (divine) voltage.

God is always taking us to the other side, to our destiny and to fulfillment.

> *'We went through fire and through water, but you brought us out to **rich fulfillment**.'* (Psalm 66:12)

Promotion!

There is no doubt that God's intent is to bring us into a larger place – promotion. He is the God of increase and change. God promises to bring us from glory to glory. *'... are being transformed into the same image from **glory to glory**, just as by the Spirit of the Lord'* (2 Corinthians 3:18).

James knew what he was talking about when he tells us to count it all joy when we encounter trials. Whenever there is a trial, a promotion will follow! In school, exams (if we pass) are always followed by a promotion. James is saying that when we are tested, God's intention is to promote us to a higher level in Him. A testing means we are being taken to the other side – a higher place.

> *'My brethren, **count it all joy** when you fall into various trials, knowing that the testing of your faith produces patience.'* (James 1:2–3)

> *'Blessed is the man who endures temptation; for when he has been approved, **he will receive the crown of life** which the Lord has promised to those who love Him.'* (James 1:12)

Peter also refers to God's ways,

> *'... the same sufferings are experienced by your brotherhood in the world. But may the God of all grace, who called us to His eternal glory by Christ Jesus, after you*

*have suffered a while, **perfect, establish, strengthen, and settle** you.'*   (1 Peter 5:9–10)

God takes us to the other side of weakness and defeat. He takes us from fear to faith, from being tormented to giving praise, from timidity to boldness, and from human respect to freedom from the opinions of people. He promotes us!

'For exaltation comes neither from the east nor from the west nor from the south. But God is the Judge: He puts down one, and exalts another.'   (Psalm 75:6–7)

Order Form

Please send me:

___ copies of *I Was Always On My Mind* ($8.00 each)

___ copies of *You Can Hear the Voice of God* ($8.00 each)

___ copies of *Breaking the Bondage Barrier – Taking the Limits Off God* ($7.00 each)

___ copies of *You Can't Use Me Today Lord . . . I Don't Feel Spiritual* ($6.00 each)

___ copies of *Enjoying God and Other Rare Events* ($3.00 each)

___ copies of *Don't Talk to Me Now Lord . . . I'm Trying to Pray!* ($4.00 each)

___ copies of *Listening to the Holy Spirit – Expecting the Miraculous* ($5.00 each)
(This is a revised printed edition of *Don't Talk to Me Now Lord . . . I'm Trying to Pray!*)

___ *Don't Underestimate the Power of Prayer* – by Marilyn Sampson ($1.00 each)

___ copies of **Medicine for the Mind** pamphlet (5 for $1.00)

___ Catalog of Cassette Tapes

I am enclosing _____ plus $2.00 for postage and handling. (Oversees orders please add an additional 20% of total.)

Mr / Mrs / Miss . . . .

Address . . . .

City, State, Zipcode . . . .

Country . . . .

Order from: Steve Sampson, PO Box 36324, Birmingham, AL 35236, USA.

If you have enjoyed this book and would like to help us to send a copy of it and many other titles to needy pastors in the **Third World**, please write for further information
or send your gift to:

Sovereign World Trust
PO Box 777, Tonbridge
Kent TN11 9XT
United Kingdom

or to the **'Sovereign World'** distributor in your country.

If sending money from outside the United Kingdom, please send an International Money Order or Foreign Bank Draft in STERLING, drawn on a **UK** bank to **Sovereign World Trust**.